THE COMPLETE BOOK OF

COCKTAILS & PUNCHES

Dedication

To my special family!
For "T" and my girls Abbie and Hannah

The Author

Sue Michalski is a cordon bleu chef who has managed bars and restaurants, and, more recently, has been involved in food and drink styling and recipe development for advertising agencies, books, magazines, and television programmes for the British Broadcasting Corporation.

Author's Acknowledgements

I would like to thank my family and friends for the enormous amount of help and back-up they have given me, especially my dear "Mutifer" for her total, undoubting support, without which this book would not have come to fruition. Also my thanks to June for her inspirational ideas.
And for their great teamwork: Blake for setting the scene, Neil for bringing the drinks to life, Jill for her finishing artistic touches, and Philip for his diplomacy and patience throughout.
It's been fun!

Sue Michalski

THE COMPLETE BOOK OF

COCKTAILS & PUNCHES

A Connoisseur's Guide to Classic and Alcohol-free Beverages

SUE MICHALSKI

AURA BOOKS

Credits

Food and drink stylist:
Sue Michalski

Photographer:
Neil Sutherland

Editor:
Philip de Ste. Croix

British adaptation:
Josephine Bacon

Designer:
Jill Coote

Photographic stylist:
Blake Minton

Production:
Ruth Arthur
Sally Connolly
Neil Randles
Karen Staff
Jonathan Tickner

Production Director:
Gerald Hughes

Typesetting:
SX Composing Ltd, England

Color reproduction:
Tien Wah Press,
Singapore

Printed and bound in Singapore by Tien Wah Press

4034
This edition published 1997 by Aura Books

Printed and bound in Singapore by Tien Wah Press
ISBN 1-85833-412-8

The author and publishers would like to thank the following people for their invaluable assistance with this book: Barbara Stewart at Surfaces in London; Ian at Parsley In Time, London; Dick at the Atlantic Bar and Grill, Regency Hotel, Piccadilly, London; Lewis and Kaye Ltd, London; and the Tortoise Courier Company.

Contents

Introduction

The very word "cocktail" seems to conjure up a feeling of relaxation and partying. There are numerous rather unconvincing stories as to how the name "cocktail" came about, but even the Oxford Dictionary concedes that its origin is unclear. Now it seems to be generally accepted as a generic term for all mixed drinks, alcoholic or otherwise. Cocktails enjoyed great popularity in the 1920s, and many of the most famous cocktails were invented then. Today, as more and more exciting ingredients are available, they are truly back in vogue.

It is because of today's trend towards more health-conscious living that I decided that this book should cover new ideas, as well as including some of the great traditional classics without which a cocktail book would be incomplete. Therefore, I have deliberately included lighter, lower alcohol cocktails and some new exciting alcohol-free concoctions for you to experiment with.

When making the recipes, do not think that you have to adhere rigidly to the measures and means that I recommend. These drinks should be fun, so if some of the recipes seem a little on the potent side, ease up a little on all the measures. For those who may like them with a bit more "kick" – let the bottle flow a little more. Experiment with the recipes, using them as a guide, and amend and adapt them to suit your own occasion and taste. For this book the quantities of spirits have been given in metric measures and fluid ounces. A "dash" is the amount of liquid released from the bottle when it is tipped with a quick flick of the wrist and then straightened again. It amounts to about half a teaspoon or 3ml.

When you start making cocktails, you may need to gain confidence and so it might be wise to measure the drinks accurately in the first instance. As you get more into the "swing of things", start to adapt them to your own taste. If you want to decrease a quantity, try measuring with a substitute item like a tablespoon or an egg cup. As long as the measure is consistent throughout any one recipe, the cocktail will still have the correct proportions and so the correct flavour. Similarly, if increasing a measurement, keep it consistent throughout.

Whichever method of mixing you use – shaken or stirred – always make sure the glasses are spotlessly clean and the cocktail served beautifully chilled. When using a shaker, half-fill

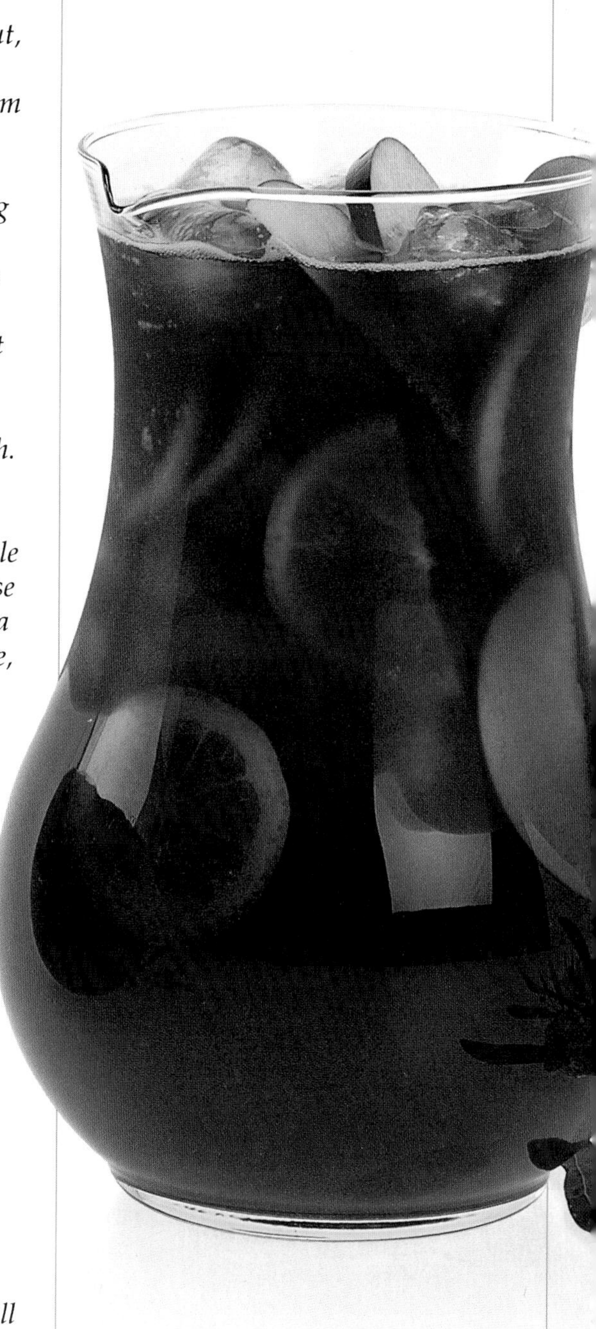

it with ice, then shake it with a very short, snappy, shaking action with plenty of gusto! Remember not to overfill the glass when serving the cocktail. Also take care not to put effervescent liquids into your shaker or blender. Just use them to top off with at the last minute, and the drink should retain all its "fizz"! Choose your garnish to enhance, rather than overwhelm, and sit back and enjoy your drink!

It may be helpful if I briefly describe the way that the book is structured. The opening pages describe equipment, glasses, ice, and how to prepare frostings, and garnishes. The book then divides into five sections. It starts with Fast Nibbles, which shows you how to make a selection of very quick, easy, and attractive light snacks to serve with drinks. The first drinks section, Classic Cocktails, covers those recipes, without which any cocktail book would be incomplete. There are some old favourites, and also some slightly less well-known classics, together with suggestions for lighter versions of some of these. The next drinks section covers Punches and Pitchers – both hot and cold, alcoholic and non-alcoholic. I have grouped these according to the seasons, so you have an interesting way to theme party drinks from spring to winter.

This brings us to the New Wave Drinks, exciting recipes using the new exotic ingredients now available. It contains some interesting flavours to tickle any taste buds. The final drinks section, Non-Alcoholic Refreshers, is devoted to alcohol-free drinks. So even if you are driving home, with a little enthusiasm and experimentation you too could be "dancing on the tables" just from the natural high of these fantastic fruit concoctions!

Cocktail Equipment

Shown here is a fairly extensive range of equipment that was used in the preparation of this book. The right equipment certainly makes preparing the cocktail and garnishes a lot easier, but it is not essential. You can still make excellent drinks with a smaller selection of utensils.

*A basic list for home use would start with a bottle opener, a corkscrew and a cocktail shaker. The standard metal variety (***7***) is probably the simplest shaker for the less experienced hand to use. It comes with a strainer built into the neck section. The two-cone "Boston" shaker (***20***) is definitely more popular with the professionals, as it proves quicker to serve, wash, and have ready for the next one! But even the shaker is not absolutely vital, as a wide-necked screw-top jar will serve the purpose, if need be. Other useful items for the home bar are a mixing glass for mixing long drinks, a blender for blending fruit, ice cream and making aerated drinks, a stainless steel strainer to hold back ice and fruit when pouring from the mixing glass, a few kitchen implements to prepare the fruit and garnishes, and some cocktail sticks to secure the finished decoration. Then all you need is enthusiasm, a spirit of adventure and a little experimentation to get you going!*

Key

1 *Ice bucket and tongs*
2 *Champagne/sparkling wine stopper*
3 *Citrus fruit reamer/ squeezer*
4 *Cocktail umbrella*
5 *Apple corer*
6 *Melon scoop/baller*
7 *Three-piece standard cocktail shaker*
8 *Salt shaker*
9 *Chopping board*
10 *Large-headed spoon strainer*
11 *Cocktail straws*
12 *Canulating knife*
13 *Citrus fruit squeezer*
14 *Barspoon*
15 *"Hawthorn" strainer*
16 *Vegetable peeler*
17 *Zester*
18 *Paring knife*
19 *Mixing glass and glass swizzle stick*
20 *Two-cone "Boston" shaker*
21 *Cup measures*
22 *Glass stirrer/muddler*
23 *Plastic stirrer/muddler*
24 *Electric blender*
25 *Spirit measures*
26 *"Waiter's friend" corkscrew/bottle opener*
27 *Nutmeg grater*

Choosing a suitable glass for your cocktail can really enhance its appearance. It requires some thought and with the wonderful choice of glassware of all sizes and shapes now available, it can prove a little difficult! I hope that the many different types of glass shown in this book will help with this decision – getting the right combination of drink and glass adds that extra touch.

Before starting to mix your cocktail, make sure that the glass chosen is spotlessly clean. It should be washed and rinsed in hot water, and well polished while still warm with a suitable cloth. If you have room in the refrigerator, try chilling the glass before serving the appropriate cocktail. It all adds to the sensation.

Illustrated here is a selection of ten basic shapes to give an idea of the sort of glass needed for the featured recipes.

Types of glasses

Champagne flute *A tall, stemmed glass suitable for champagne and sparkling wine drinks. It holds 200-250ml/6-8 fl oz.*

Brandy balloon *For straight brandy and brandy-based drinks. It holds between 175-750ml/6-24 fl oz, depending on its volume.*

Large goblet/Wine glass *These glasses vary greatly in shape and size. You can use them for serving simple wine spritzers or for some of the ice cream drinks in the case of the larger glasses, as they hold between 250-500ml/8-14 fl oz.*

Tumbler *A sloping-sided tumbler such as this normally holds between 125-250ml/4-8 fl oz. It is suitable for cocktails such as a Bloodshot, and for serving fruit juices.*

Double cocktail glass *A large, rounded cocktail glass which is very useful for serving cream-based cocktails such as a Coconut Melon. It has a capacity of approx. 175-300ml/6-10 fl oz.*
Old Fashioned *A short, straight-sided tumbler which holds between 125-250ml/ 4-8 fl oz of drink. It is good for serving fresh fruit juices on their own and, of course, for serving the drink from which it derives its name – an Old Fashioned cocktail.*
Cocktail/Martini glass *A stemmed, wide-rimmed, triangular-shaped glass normally used for cocktails such as an Alexander and, of course, the Martini. It has a capacity of between 125-175ml/4-6 fl oz.*
Liqueur glass *This is ideal for serving short, straight drink measures of between 30-60ml/1-2 fl oz.*

Collins *A tall straight-sided glass wih a large capacity of between 300-500ml/10-14 fl oz. It is excellent for long drinks like a Tom Collins or a Zombie.*
Highball *A smaller glass than a Collins holding between 250-300ml/8-10 fl oz. It is possibly the most useful general type of glass, and is ideal for many drinks like a Harvey Wallbanger and Iced Tea.*

Not illustrated here, but used for certain recipes are:
Pousse-café glass *A short-stemmed, narrow, straight-sided glass, excellent for the layered drinks from which it takes its name. It holds approx 125-175ml/4-6 fl oz.*
Irish coffee glass *A heat-resistant glass with a handle, generally holding between 250-300ml/8-10 fl oz.*

Key
1 *Champagne flute*
2 *Brandy balloon*
3 *Large goblet/Wine glass*
4 *Tumbler*
5 *Double cocktail glass*
6 *Old Fashioned*
7 *Cocktail/Martini glass*
8 *Liqueur glass*
9 *Collins*
10 *Highball*

Preparing and Using Ice

Many cocktails have to be served properly chilled. Ice, of course, plays a very important role here. Whether it is shaken with the ingredients and then strained away, or simply added to the drink, the ice need not be plain. Here are some ideas for creating decorative effects with ice. For a start, it can be made in a variety of shapes, flavours, and colours. You do this by using shaped ice moulds, like the one illustrated, and adding flavouring agents, such as syrups, to the water. Ice can be cubed, cracked – achieved by wrapping the cubes in a clean cloth and hitting with a mallet or rolling pin – or crushed, when it is broken up even more finely. Special machines can be bought to crush ice, but you do not

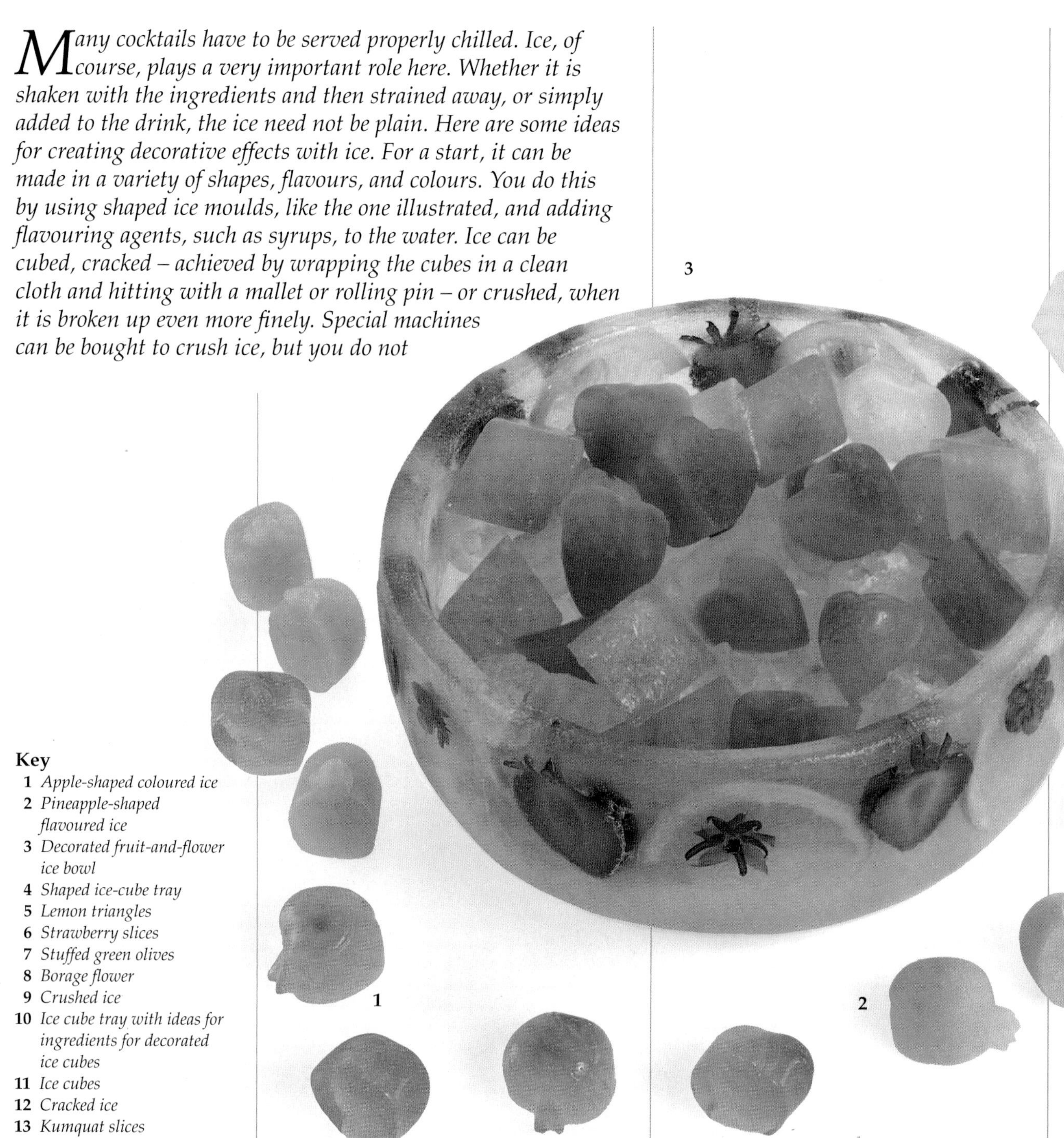

Key
1 *Apple-shaped coloured ice*
2 *Pineapple-shaped flavoured ice*
3 *Decorated fruit-and-flower ice bowl*
4 *Shaped ice-cube tray*
5 *Lemon triangles*
6 *Strawberry slices*
7 *Stuffed green olives*
8 *Borage flower*
9 *Crushed ice*
10 *Ice cube tray with ideas for ingredients for decorated ice cubes*
11 *Ice cubes*
12 *Cracked ice*
13 *Kumquat slices*
14 *Lime triangles*

need to have one. Simply keep hammering at the cracked ice until it is at the consistency you require.

Why not make your own "ice bucket" using a decorated ice bowl? It makes an attractive centrepiece for a table. You will find instructions on how to do this on page 77. Alternatively, decorate ice cubes by half-filling the ice-tray with water, freezing it, then adding your decoration on top of the ice section, topping off the tray with more water, and freezing again. These look very pretty floating in colourless or light-coloured drinks!

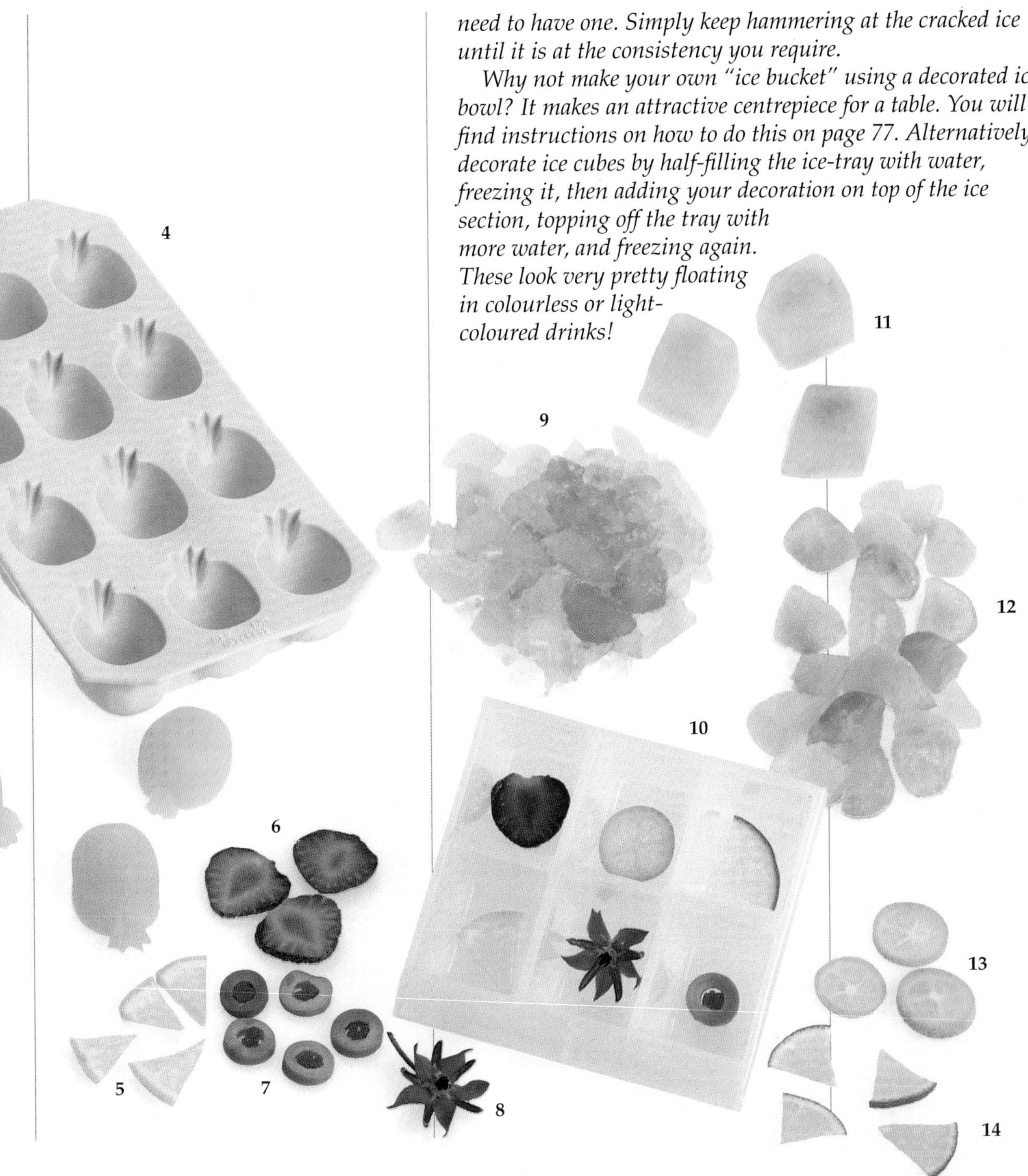

Decorating and Frosting the Glass

Frosting is a technique that allows you to coat the rim of a glass with a sweet or savoury flavouring. You will find instructions on how to do it on page 40. It can be very enjoyable to sip a drink from a frosted glass, and to let the different taste sensations mingle in your mouth. A variety of ingredients may be used to frost the rim. As a rule, if you are using frostings such as salt or celery salt, use lemon or lime juice to moisten the rim. For sweeter frostings, use lightly beaten egg white.

To dye sugar and coconut, toss the ingredients with powdered food colouring. Other alternatives are

Key

1 *Ground almond frosting*
2 *Dyed blue sugar frosting*
3 *Dyed red sugar frosting*
4 *Medium-coarse rock salt frosting*
5 *Ground nutmeg frosting*
6 *Dyed yellow dried coconut frosting*
7 *Dyed pink sugar frosting*

to mix instant coffee, chocolate powder or cinnamon with sugar as a frosting.

In the case of savoury frostings, such as the salt used with a Salty Dog or Margarita, the cocktail is usually drunk through the frosting, whereas the sweeter ones are often used more for decoration and so may be served with straws.

Also displayed here are a few of the accessories that can be used to decorate a drink: cocktail umbrellas, straws of all shapes and sizes, coloured stirrers and sparklers. They are not appropriate all the time, but if you are having a special celebration, why not go for it?

Citrus Garnishes

Citrus fruits are tremendously versatile ingredients when it comes to garnishing cocktails. You can use just a simple slice on the edge of the glass, or experiment with more complicated decorations, such as spiralling peel or kumquat "lily" flowers. Instructions as to how to make these and other garnishes shown on subsequent pages will be found in the step-by-step sequences featured throughout the book.

Choose firm, thin-skinned, unblemished and preferably unwaxed fruit. Always wash the fruit before preparing the garnishes and make sure you use a sharp paring knife.

Displayed here is a varied selection of garnishes made mainly from oranges, lemons and limes. However, any citrus fruit can be used. You simply adapt these ideas to the fruit that you prefer. With their orangey-red flesh, blood oranges can look very striking. Ugli fruit, grapefruits, clementines, satsumas – all are suitable. Just experiment a little.

You can make a drink look really appealing simply by floating a couple of star shapes cut from some peel on the top of it. Let your imagination play its part.

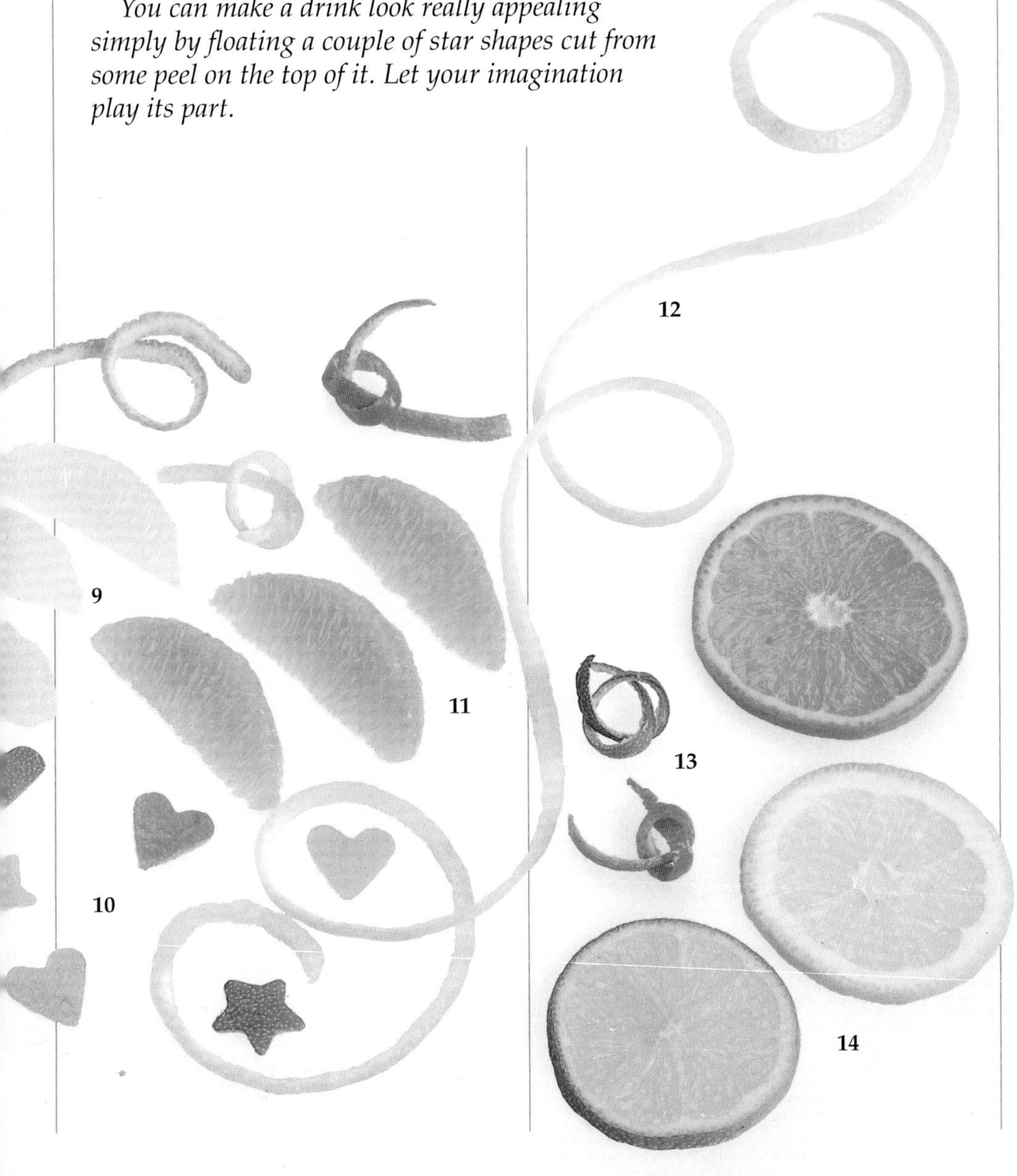

12

9

11

13

10

14

Key

1 *Long lime peel spiral*
2 *Lemon peel knot*
3 *Half orange and lime slice/spiral, for curling around the outside of a glass*
4 *Canulated orange, lemon, and lime "wheel" slices*
5 *Kumquat "lily" flowers*
6 *Short canulated orange peel*
7 *Quarter and half slices of orange, lemon and lime*
8 *Medium length canulated orange peel*
9 *Grapefruit segments*
10 *Citrus peel shapes*
11 *Orange segments*
12 *Long piece of canulated lemon peel, for tying a lemon peel bow*
13 *Lime and orange peel knots*
14 *Plain orange, lemon and lime slices*

Mixed Fruit Garnishes

Key
1 *Double citrus slice twist*
2 *Orange and cherry sail*
3 *Triple citrus slice twist*
4 *Coloured cocktail cherries*
5 *Stemmed cocktail cherries*
6 *Stemmed maraschino cherries*
7 *Lemon twist with maraschino cherry*
8 *Triple fresh raspberry stick*

The garnish on a cocktail should be there to enhance its appearance, rather than disguise it. So bear in mind the size of the glass and the overall scale of the drink you are preparing, when selecting a garnish from among the ideas illustrated. Fruits are not always in season, but you can use both fresh and preserved ingredients, depending on what is available. Just a simple string of fresh redcurrants hung over the edge of the glass, or a tiny bunch of frosted grapes can be all that is needed

to create a wonderfully effective garnish.

Mixing complementary colours and textures, and choosing fruits that echo the drink's ingredients are all part of the art of creating the right finishing touch.

For most cocktails it is usually safer to err on the side of simplicity when selecting a garnish. Otherwise the drink will look way over the top and almost unapproachable. You are serving a drink, not a snack!

9 *Blueberry and lemon twist*
10 *Pairs of seedless grapes*
11 *Various coloured melon balls*
12 *Multicoloured melon ball sticks*
13 *Strawberry fan*
14 *Stemmed fresh cherries*
15 *Half a strawberry fan*
16 *Strawberry slice with hulls*
17 *Slices of banana with the skin on*

10

13

17

15

14

16

11

12

9

Fruit and Vegetable Garnishes

The more "tropical" cocktails that use exotic ingredients, like a Piña Colada, really seem to invite you to be somewhat "over the top" in their presentation. The choice of all the wonderful colours and shapes, from papaya, pineapple, coconuts, starfruit and mango to the wondrous contrasting green-and-black flesh of a kiwi fruit, are so beguiling that even the strongest willed person cannot help being tempted a little when so spoiled for choice!

Simple everyday fruits, such as an apple, can also make a very attractive garnish when chevroned, while tiny cherry tomato skins make beautifully dainty roses. You just need a little patience and care to make them. When floated on a canulated slice of cucumber on the surface of a drink, they make a beautiful decorative garnish. No store cupboard would be complete without stuffed green olives and neither would the most famous cocktail of all – a Martini.

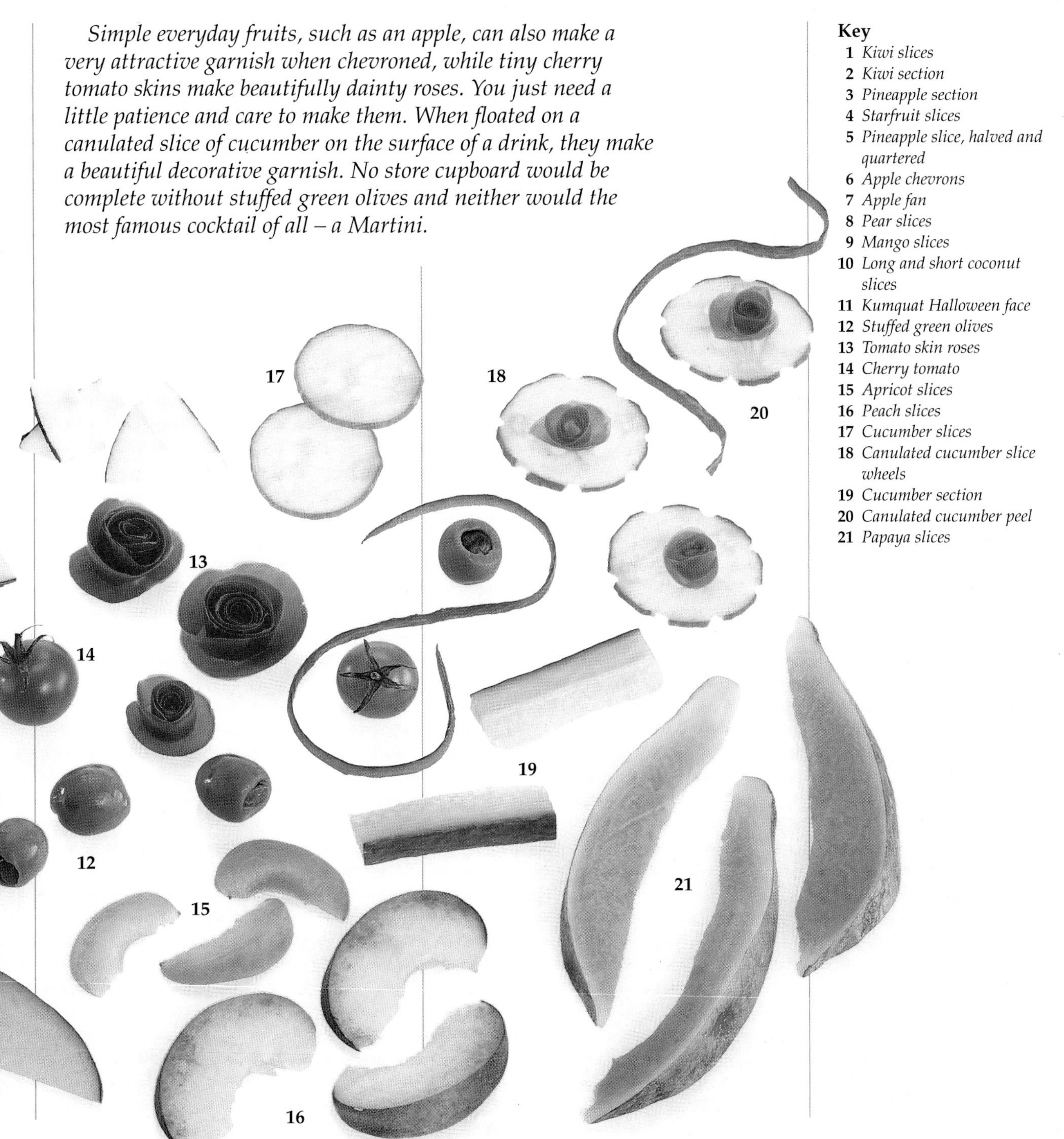

Key

1 *Kiwi slices*
2 *Kiwi section*
3 *Pineapple section*
4 *Starfruit slices*
5 *Pineapple slice, halved and quartered*
6 *Apple chevrons*
7 *Apple fan*
8 *Pear slices*
9 *Mango slices*
10 *Long and short coconut slices*
11 *Kumquat Halloween face*
12 *Stuffed green olives*
13 *Tomato skin roses*
14 *Cherry tomato*
15 *Apricot slices*
16 *Peach slices*
17 *Cucumber slices*
18 *Canulated cucumber slice wheels*
19 *Cucumber section*
20 *Canulated cucumber peel*
21 *Papaya slices*

Flowers, Leaves, Herbs and Spices

There are many ways in which the flowers and leaves of plants can be incorporated into a decoration for a drink. For sheer simplicity, the natural beauty of a single flower, such as an orchid or a rose, may be all that is needed. Or try floating petals on top of the drink – the effect is magical.

If you decide to decorate a drink with fruit, such as a strawberry, why not complete the picture by adding tiny strawberry flowers and leaves as well? The same principle applies when using pineapple pieces – pineapple leaves with their dramatic shape add the finishing touch to the garnish.

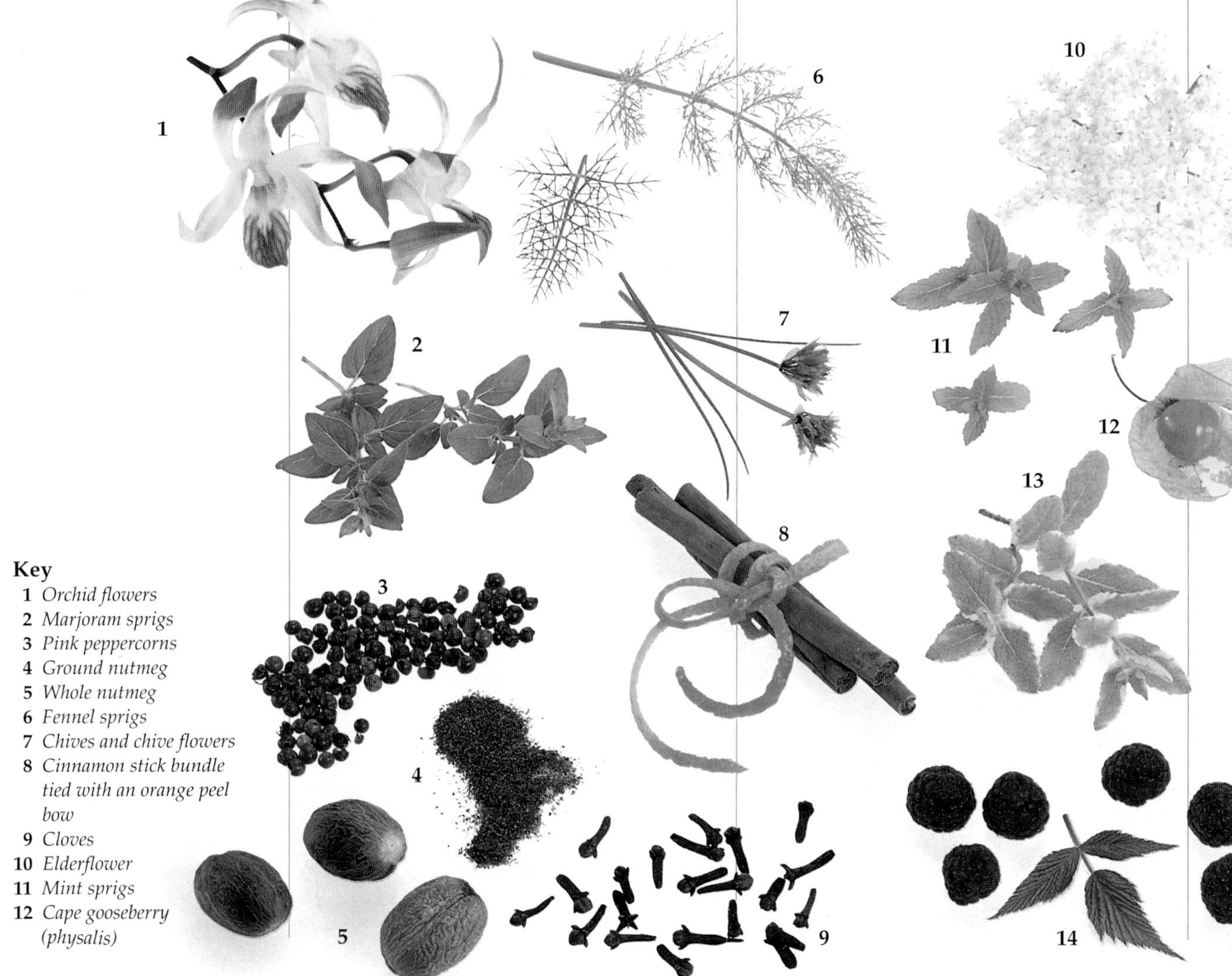

Key

1 *Orchid flowers*
2 *Marjoram sprigs*
3 *Pink peppercorns*
4 *Ground nutmeg*
5 *Whole nutmeg*
6 *Fennel sprigs*
7 *Chives and chive flowers*
8 *Cinnamon stick bundle tied with an orange peel bow*
9 *Cloves*
10 *Elderflower*
11 *Mint sprigs*
12 *Cape gooseberry (physalis)*

Do not feel you have to restrict your use of leaves to sweet or aromatic drinks; you can use the celery leaves on top of a celery stick in drinks of a more savoury nature like a Bloody Mary, for instance.

Herbs and herb flowers combine beautifully both in appearance and in aroma if used in mulling – bay leaves combined with a variety of spices really add that little hint of the unknown to the finished drink. Try using cinnamon, cloves, nutmeg, peppercorns – in the right place such spices can prove the pièce de résistance.

13 *Variegated applemint sprigs*
14 *Raspberries and leaves*
15 *Redcurrants and leaves*
16 *Strawberries with flowers and leaves*
17 *Basil sprigs*
18 *Miniature rose, rosebud, and hulls*
19 *Thyme sprigs and flowers*
20 *Rose petals*
21 *Celery stick with leaves*
22 *Pineapple leaves*
23 *Bay leaves*

Cheese and Salmon Savouries

Cherry Tomatoes with Basil

▼ **Serves 20**

10 cherry tomatoes
125-175ml/4-6 fl oz cream cheese
4 sprigs of basil, stalks removed, chopped finely
Dash of Tabasco sauce, salt and pepper

Cut the tomatoes in half and scoop out the seeds. Turn the tomatoes upside down on paper towels and leave to drain. Mix the cream cheese, chopped basil and Tabasco sauce together. Season to taste. Place the mixture into a piping bag with a fluted nozzle and pipe swirls into the tomatoes. Decorate with extra sprigs of basil.

Smoked Salmon Diamonds

Serves 20 ▶

8 thin slices buttered brown bread, crusts removed
225g/8 oz smoked salmon slices
A small jar of "mock caviar" (pink-dyed cod's roe)
Fennel sprigs

Lay the smoked salmon slices on to the bread, cut into diamond shapes, and place a small cluster of "caviar" in the centre. Decorate with tiny fennel sprigs.

Gorgonzola Pecans

◀ **Serves 20**

40 pecan halves
175g/6 oz Gorgonzola cheese (or any creamy blue cheese)

Cream the cheese with a wooden spoon. Sandwich the pecan halves together using about a teaspoon of the creamed Gorgonzola. Decorate with little wedges of lemon or lime.

Salmon, Spinach, and Cream Cheese Pinwheels

◀ **Serves 20**

8 thin slices of brown bread, crusts removed
125g/4 oz very young spinach leaves (use sorrel or watercress if not available)
175g/6 oz smoked salmon slices
125-175g/4-6 oz cream cheese
Lemon or lime juice
Salt and pepper

Lay out the bread and flatten each slice by rolling with a rolling pin. Spread the cream cheese evenly over each slice, then cover with the small spinach leaves. Lay the salmon on top, brush with lemon or lime juice, and season with salt and pepper. Roll up like a Swiss roll, being careful not to roll too tightly and so squeeze out the filling. Pack tightly together in a box, cover with clingfilm, and chill for at least an hour. Then slice into 1.5cm/ half-inch-thick slices.

Date Splits

▼ **Serves 20**

20 fresh dates, cut down the length on one side, stoned
225g/8 oz cream cheese
A little milk
40 toasted split almonds

Soften the cream cheese a little in a bowl, working it with a fork until smooth, and add a little milk to make it workable. Put into a piping bag fitted with a fluted nozzle, and pipe the cream cheese into the split dates, filling the date lengthways. Place two split almonds at an angle on each. Large white or black grapes can be used as an alternative to the dates.

Smoked Chicken and Watermelon

▼ **Serves 20**

300g/10 oz smoked chicken breast
20 watermelon balls (about 1.5cm/½ in)

Cut the chicken into 20 bite-size pieces. Thread a piece of chicken followed by a watermelon ball onto each stick.

Grapes with Brie or Stilton

◀ **Serves 20**

125g/4 oz ripe Brie cheese
125g/4 oz mature Stilton
10 large black grapes, halved and seeded
10 large white grapes, halved and seeded

Cut the Brie and Stilton into 1.5cm/half-inch cubes, 10 of each. Thread half a white grape onto a cocktail stick followed by a piece of Brie and then another grape. Do the same with the black grapes and the Stilton pieces.

Cucumber, Prawn and Melon

▼ **Serves 20**

20 slices of canulated cucumber – cut each slice from the middle to the outer edge
20 prawns, peeled
20 1.5cm/half-inch watermelon balls

Thread one piece of each of the cucumber, prawns, and watermelon onto a cocktail stick, with the cucumber twisting around the prawn and melon.

Tomato, Mozzarella, and Black Olives

Serves 20 ▶

3 large tomatoes, peeled
100g/4 oz firm mozzarella cheese
10 large olives, pitted and halved

Cut the tomatoes in half, remove the seeds and cut into 1.5cm/½ in squares. Then cut the mozzarella into 1.5cm/½ in cubes and thread a piece of tomato, then cheese, and finally an olive onto a cocktail stick.

Parma Ham Wraps

▼ **Serves 20**

175g/6 oz Parma ham – thinly sliced
2 figs
1 mango
2 kiwi fruit
A wedge of ripe melon

Cut the figs into bite-sized pieces. Seed the melon and scoop into balls. Remove the seed from the mango, and cut the flesh into wedge slices. Skin and cube the kiwi fruit. Cut the ham into 2.5cm/1 in strips, and secure around each piece of fruit.

Marinated Halibut Sticks

▲ **Serves 20**

A large red pepper – halved, seeded, and cut into 1.5cm/½ in squares
225g/8 oz boned halibut, skinned
Juice of a lemon
Juice of a lime
Half a clove of garlic, crushed
Salt and pepper
A tablespoon of tarragon, finely chopped
A bunch of finely chopped watercress
125ml/4 fl oz mayonnaise
125ml/4 fl oz fresh cream

Mix the juice of the lemon and lime with the tarragon, garlic, salt, and pepper. Cube the halibut into 1.5cm/½ in cubes, and put into this marinade. Cover and leave for at least two hours. Meanwhile mix together the watercress, mayonnaise and cream, seasoning to taste. Put a piece of pepper and marinated fish on to each cocktail stick, and serve with the watercress mayonnaise.

Smoked Chicken Bites

▼ **Serves 20**

250g/8 oz smoked chicken meat, minced
125g/4 oz softened butter
1 tablespoon chopped chives
1 teaspoon mango chutney
6 tablespoons finely chopped parsley

In a blender combine the chicken, butter, chives and chutney. Season to taste. Shape into small balls and roll them in the chopped parsley. Cover and chill well before serving.

Filled Pastry Boats

▼ **Serves 20**

20 savoury mini-pastry cases, various shapes
20 mini croustade cases
1 can smoked oysters, drained
1 can smoked mussels, drained
2 small jars mock caviar, 1 red and 1 black
1 lime and 1 lemon
Fresh dill

Fill the pastry cases with one oyster and one mussel, decorate with tiny lemon and lime triangles and a sprig of dill. Fill the croustades with black and red caviar, allowing a fairly generous amount for each.
Put a tiny cluster of contrasting coloured caviar on the top of each as decoration.

Pumpernickel Swirls

◀ **Serves 20**

5 slices of pumpernickel or rye bread
250g/8 oz salmon or smoked trout mousse
Salmon roe or "mock caviar"
1 lime

With a 2.5cm/1 in cutter, cut 4 circles from each slice of bread. Put the fish mousse into a piping bag fitted with a fluted nozzle, and pipe swirls on to each piece. Top with salmon roe or "mock caviar" and small pieces of fresh lime.

Tandoori Chicken and Minted Cucumber Dip

Serves 20

250g/8 oz boneless chicken breast
125g/4 oz yogurt
1 tablespoon tandoori powder or paste
1 teaspoon garam masala
1 teaspoon chilli powder
Juice of a lemon
Salt and pepper

For the dip:
A quarter of a cucumber – finely chopped and drained
125g/4 oz yogurt
2 tablespoons chopped fresh mint

Mix the yogurt, tandoori powder/paste, chilli powder, garam masala and lemon juice together. Cut the chicken into small bite-size pieces and put them into the marinade. Cover and chill for at least four hours, preferably overnight.

Make the dip by stirring together the yogurt and mint, and folding in the chopped cucumber. Season to taste. Take the chicken out of the marinade. Put the pieces on a grill pan and cook under the preheated grill on its highest setting for about ten minutes, turning them to cook evenly. Spear onto cocktail sticks and serve with the dip.

Quail Eggs

Serves 20

20 quail eggs
Celery salt

Boil the quail eggs for four minutes, then plunge into ice-cold water. Serve them shelled or unshelled with the celery salt.

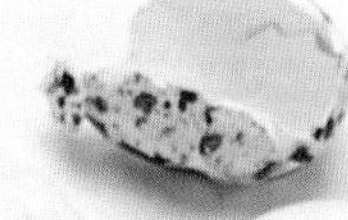

Devils

Serves 20

175g/6 oz prunes, ready to eat, pitted (20 prunes)
250g/8 oz rindless streaky bacon, approx. 10 rashers

Stretch each bacon rasher by putting it on a board and running the back of a knife along its length. Cut the bacon in half and roll it around each prune, securing with a wooden cocktail stick. Put the rolls on a non-stick baking sheet, place in a preheated oven and bake at 200°C/400°F/Gas Mark 6 for 15 minutes. Drain on a wire rack and serve warm.

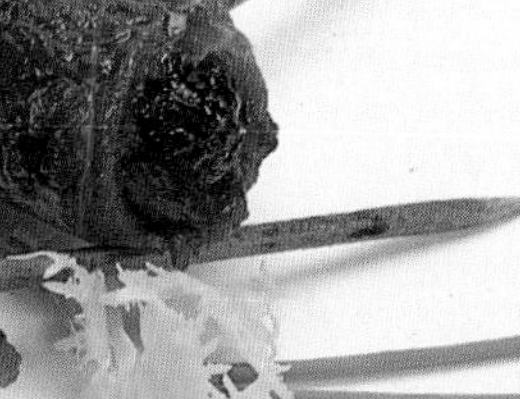

Surprise Mini Meringues

Serves 20

40 halves of mini meringue shells
375ml/12 fl oz whipping cream
60g/2 oz strawberries – puréed in the blender
2 teaspoons coffee essence
20 mini paper cases
Toasted flaked almonds and strawberry pieces as decoration
(Recipe continued below)

Quick Truffles

Serves 20

125g/4 oz cream cheese
300g/10 oz sifted icing sugar
60g/2 oz ground almonds
250g/8 oz plain chocolate
A tablespoon of dark rum or brandy
To coat – cocoa powder, chocolate vermicelli, desiccated coconut
Mini paper cases

Soften the cream cheese with an electric whisk in a bowl. Then gradually add the icing sugar and ground almonds. Melt the chocolate in a bowl in a microwave oven or over hot water, stir in the rum or brandy, and add to the cream cheese mixture, mixing it in quickly and evenly. Roll into small balls and coat in the cocoa, coconut or vermicelli strands. Put into paper cases and chill well before serving.

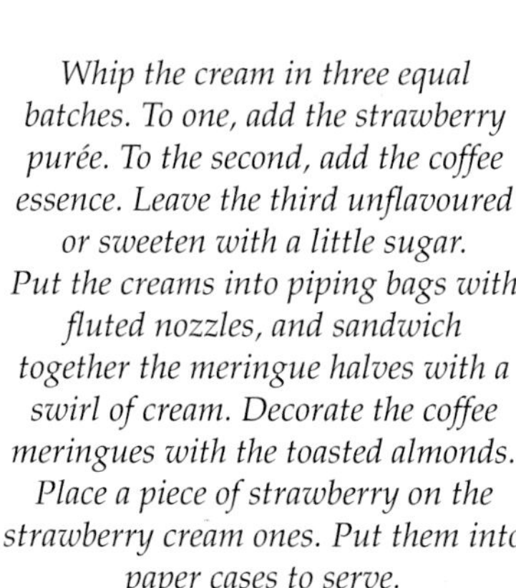

Whip the cream in three equal batches. To one, add the strawberry purée. To the second, add the coffee essence. Leave the third unflavoured or sweeten with a little sugar. Put the creams into piping bags with fluted nozzles, and sandwich together the meringue halves with a swirl of cream. Decorate the coffee meringues with the toasted almonds. Place a piece of strawberry on the strawberry cream ones. Put them into paper cases to serve.

Chocolate-Dipped Fruits

◀ **Serves 20**

20 small strawberries
20 kumquats
20 lychees
4 small slices of fresh pineapple
250g/8 oz dark bitter chocolate
250g/8 oz white chocolate

Cut the pineapple into chunks and skin the lychees and leave both to drain on paper towels. Melt each type of chocolate separately in the microwave or in bowls over hot water. Then dip the ends of the kumquats, strawberries, and lychees and part of each pineapple chunk into the melted chocolates. Put the dipped fruits onto trays lined with wax paper until the chocolate has hardened completely and serve.

Golden Grapes

◀ **Serves 20**

20 white grapes, with a little stalk attached to each
250g/8 oz granulated sugar
A little water
A large bowl of ice water
An oiled baking sheet

Place the sugar and water in a heavy-bottomed pan. Dissolve the sugar over a low heat and boil until it turns a golden caramel colour. Put the base of the pan into the bowl of ice water to stop the mixture from cooking further. Then dip the grapes into the caramel (being careful not to let it touch your fingers). Then leave them to set on the oiled baking sheet.

Fresh Fruit Tartlets

▼ **Serves 20**

20 mini sweet pastry cases – baked
A small can (250ml/8 oz) of custard
20 small strawberries – cut into decorative fan-shapes
30 raspberries – halved
A few sprigs of redcurrants and blackcurrants
Redcurrant jelly
A squeeze of lemon juice

Put a teaspoon of custard into each pastry case, and arrange a selection of the fruit on top. Melt the redcurrant jelly with the lemon juice, and brush over the tartlets. Decorate with strawberry flowers, if available.

Lemon, lime and cherry sail

It is best to use stemmed maraschino cherries for a prettier result. Choose a lemon and lime of similar size (so that the garnish when finished will look in proportion). Then, using a sharp knife, cut a thin slice from each of the citrus fruits.

Place the lime slice on top of the lemon slice and a maraschino cherry on top of these. Thread the cocktail stick through the two slices of fruit on one side, through the cherry, and finally out through the other side of the fruit slice, securing the garnish together neatly. The completed garnish may be balanced across the edge of the glass or just placed in the finished cocktail.

Gin and French

45ml/1½ fl oz gin
45ml/1½ fl oz French dry vermouth
Soda water or tonic water
Ice
Glass: Highball
Garnish: A sprig of mint and a sliver of lemon peel

Shake the gin, vermouth and ice together, then strain into the glass.
For a long cool drink, mix the gin and vermouth together in an ice-filled highball glass, top off with soda water or tonic water. Finish by adding a sprig of mint.

Kamikaze

60ml/2 fl oz vodka
30ml/1 fl oz lemon juice
2 teaspoons of lime cordial
Ice
Glass: Cocktail
Garnish: A twist of lemon peel and a cocktail cherry

Pour all the ingredients into a shaker, shake and strain into a glass.

Americano

45ml/1½ fl oz Campari
45ml/1½ fl oz sweet vermouth
Soda water
Ice
Glass: Old fashioned
Garnish: A slice of orange, or a lemon, lime and cherry twist

Pour the Campari and vermouth into an ice-filled glass. Stir in soda water to taste.

Blue Negligée

30ml/1 fl oz ouzo
30ml/1 fl oz Parfait Amour
30ml/1 fl oz green Chartreuse
Ice – crushed
Glass: Cocktail
Garnish: A slice of lemon

Shake all the ingredients together, then strain into a glass half-filled with ice.

BARMAN'S NOTES

An apéritif – this is a drink that should stimulate the palate, getting one's senses buzzing in anticipation for what is to come next. The word is derived from the Latin "aperire", meaning to open, which is why it has become associated with a drink served at the beginning of the meal. On the market now are a vast array of commercial apéritifs – a lot of them wine-based with various flavourings.
Wines have definitely become more fashionable in recent years, with champagne and sparkling wines, the dry whites and a spritzer all being pleasant choices for a lighter start. Some cocktails and liqueurs are also still popular, especially the less sweet varieties, and the aniseed-based ones. Featured on these pages are some excellent appetite arousers. If you fancy something different, the traditional Martini (page 46), gin & tonic, a whisky sour (page 52) or a Margarita (page 90) offer a nice way to get an event off its starting blocks.

Gin and Tonic

60ml/2 fl oz gin
125ml/5 fl oz tonic water
Ice
Glass: Highball
Garnish: Slice of lemon

Pour the gin into the serving glass, half-filled with ice, and top off with the tonic water to taste.

Short orange peel twist

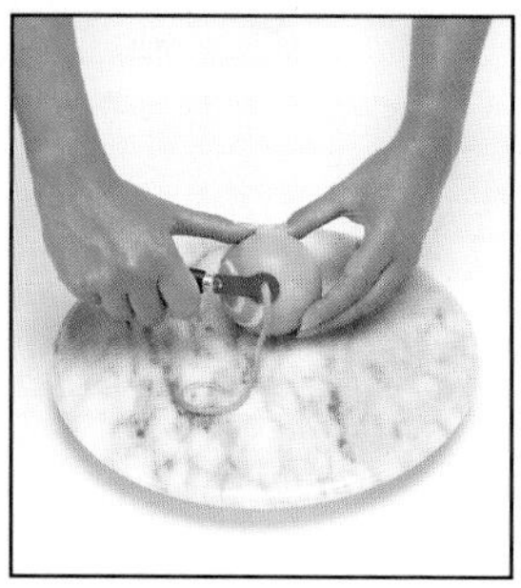

Choose a firm, thin-skinned orange. Wash and dry the fruit. Using a canulating knife, take off a continuous strip of peel about the length of half the orange.

Take the length of orange peel, and with a sharp knife scrape off any of the remaining pith, as this may create a bitter taste. Then twist the peel around between your thumb and forefinger, and drop it into the cocktail.

Harvey Wallbanger

45ml/1½ fl oz vodka
30ml/1 fl oz Galliano
Fresh orange juice
Ice
Glass: Highball
Garnish: A slice of lime

In a glass half-filled with ice pour in the vodka and Galliano. Top off with orange juice to taste, then stir and garnish.

Surfrider

75ml/2½ fl oz vodka
45ml/1½ fl oz sweet vermouth
Juice of an orange
A squeeze of lime
1 teaspoon of grenadine
Ice
Glass: Goblet
Garnish: A slice of orange and a maraschino cherry

Pour all the ingredients into a shaker, shake, strain into the glass, then garnish.

Long Island Iced Tea

30ml/1 fl oz vodka
30ml/1 fl oz light rum
30ml/1 fl oz tequila
30ml/1 fl oz gin
15ml/½ fl oz Triple Sec Curaçao
30ml/1 fl oz lemon juice
2 teaspoons icing sugar
90ml/3 fl oz cola
Ice
Glass: Highball
Garnish: A lemon twist and mint leaves

Pour all the ingredients into a highball glass half-filled with ice, stir well and garnish.

Patricia

30ml/1 fl oz vodka
30ml/1 fl oz sweet vermouth
30ml/1 fl oz Cointreau
Glass: Cocktail
Garnish: A twist of lemon or orange peel

Stir all the ingredients together and add the garnish.

BARMAN'S NOTES

Vodka has long enjoyed considerable worldwide popularity as a base for cocktails, mainly because of its neutral character. Its lack of smell and flavour allows it to mix smoothly with other ingredients without altering their taste, yet giving the drink that extra "kick".
The Russians like to say that vodka was invented by them in the 12th century in the Russian fort of Viataka. (Others believe it to have originated in Prussia in the 11th century.) A strong colourless spirit, very similar in nature, was certainly drunk there at that time. It was originally named "Zhiznennia voda" which translates as "water of life". This was abbreviated affectionately to the word "vodka" or "wodka" (in Polish) meaning "little water"! Vodka is generally a cleaner, purer spirit than (say) brandy, as in its manufacturing process certain oils and chemical compounds called congenerics are removed by filtration. These congenerics give spirits their undesirable after-effect if taken in excess, and so their removal means that the spirit is less likely to inflict retribution on those who overindulge. So, although vodka has a high spirit level, it could be said to be slightly "kinder" to drink!

Frosting the glass with salt

Wash and dry the glass thoroughly. Pour medium/coarse salt into a dish wide enough to accommodate the circumference of the glass rim. Cut a thin lemon or lime wedge, gently squeeze it between your thumb and forefinger and wipe it around the whole rim of the glass.

Holding the glass firmly upside down, dip the moistened rim into the salt, covering the rim evenly. If the frosting looks uneven, just repeat the process.

Salty Dog

60ml/2 fl oz vodka
Fresh grapefruit juice
Ice
Glass: Highball
Garnish: Frost the glass with salt, and add a wedge of lemon

Pour the vodka over the ice in the salt-frosted glass. Top off with grapefruit juice and garnish.

Blue Lagoon

45ml/1½ fl oz vodka
45ml/1½ fl oz blue Curaçao
Lemon-lime soda
Ice
Glass: Long-stemmed goblet
Garnish: Cocktail cherries

Pour the vodka and Curaçao into an ice-filled glass, stir, and top off with the lemon-lime soda. Garnish.

Sea Waves

45ml/1½ fl oz vodka
15ml/½ fl oz dry vermouth
15ml/½ fl oz blue Curaçao
15ml/½ fl oz Galliano
Ice
Glass: Cocktail or wine goblet
Garnish: Maraschino cherries

Pour the ingredients into a glass half-filled with ice, stir well and garnish.

Perfect John

60ml/2 fl oz vodka
30ml/1 fl oz Triple Sec Curaçao
125ml/4 fl oz freshly squeezed orange juice
Ice
Glass: Highball
Garnish: A slice of orange

Half-fill the glass with ice, and add the vodka and triple sec. Top off with the orange juice and garnish.

BARMAN'S NOTES

There is not room here to illustrate all the famous recipes for vodka-based cocktails. However, if you want to experiment further, try some of the following:

Screwdriver
60ml/2 fl oz vodka
150ml/5 fl oz freshly squeezed orange juice
Ice
Glass: Highball
Garnish: An orange wheel

Half-fill the glass with ice and add the vodka. Top off with the orange juice.

Fuzzy Navel
30ml/1 fl oz vodka
30ml/1 fl oz peach schnapps
125ml/4 fl oz freshly squeezed orange juice
Ice
Glass: Highball
Garnish: A slice of peach and a slice of orange

Mix all the ingredients together in the serving glass half-filled with ice, and garnish.

Sex on the Beach
30ml/1 fl oz vodka
30ml/1 fl oz peach schnapps
60ml/2 fl oz orange juice
60ml/2 fl oz cranberry juice
Ice
Glass: Highball
Garnish: Slice of orange and a cherry

Pour all the ingredients into the serving glass half-filled with ice. Stir well then garnish.

Grating nutmeg

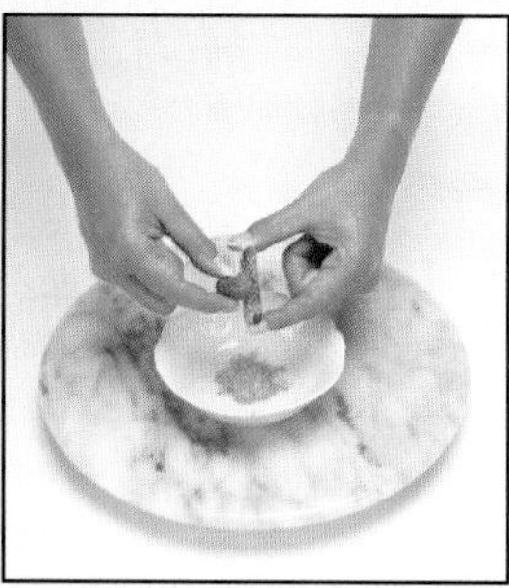

Freshly grated nutmeg sprinkled or grated directly over the finished cocktail adds that extra little something to the appearance and flavour of the drink. Nutmeg is very hard and to grate it you must run it firmly to and fro over a very fine grater. Special tiny nutmeg graters can be bought for the job.

Chocolate curls or shavings

Chocolate curls can be made quite simply by using an ordinary vegetable peeler. Hold the chocolate firmly in one hand and peel the chocolate with the peeler. The more pressure you use, the more the chocolate will form curls rather than thin shavings. Use this to garnish the top of the cocktail.

Moscow Mule

60ml/2 fl oz vodka
30ml/1 fl oz lemon or lime juice
Ginger beer
Ice
Glass: Highball
Garnish: A slice of lime

Pour the vodka and lime or lemon juice into the glass half-filled with ice. Stir, top off with ginger beer, then garnish.

Galway Gray

45ml/1½ fl oz vodka
30ml/1 fl oz white crème de cacao
30ml/1 fl oz Cointreau
15ml/½ fl oz lime juice
Fresh cream
Glass: Cocktail
Garnish: Grated orange peel

Stir all the ingredients together, except for the cream. Then float the cream on the top and garnish.

White Russian

30ml/1 fl oz vodka
15ml/½ fl oz Kahlua coffee liqueur
15ml/½ fl oz white crème de cacao
45ml/1 measure cream
Ice – cubed and cracked
Glass: Highball
Garnish: Freshly grated chocolate and nutmeg

Shake all the ingredients together with the cracked ice. Then strain into the glass half-filled with ice cubes, and sprinkle with the chocolate and nutmeg.

Road Runner

60ml/2 fl oz vodka
30ml/1 fl oz amaretto liqueur
30ml/1 fl oz coconut milk
Ice
Glass: Cocktail
Garnish: Freshly grated nutmeg

Combine the ingredients in a shaker, shake, and strain into the glass. Garnish with a dusting of nutmeg.

BARMAN'S NOTES

The art of distilling a neutral spirit from starchy substances, such as maize, potatoes or rye, soon became common knowledge throughout Russia. The technique spread into Finland and then to Poland. By the 16th century many Poles knew how to produce vodka, and numerous families produced their own vodka, flavouring it with various herbs and fruits.

In around 1820, a Russian family set up a firm to produce vodka, and its name has become synonymous with this spirit – Smirnoff. The real stimulus to Smirnoff's rise to fame came when the company was awarded the royal monopoly to supply vodka and vodka-based drinks to the Imperial court by Tzar Alexander III. Apparently this was a reward for a clever promotional stunt devised by the head of the company. He had a drinking pavillion built at a fair – for waiters he hired entertainers to dress as bears, while a real bear assisted them at the bar! It had been trained to taste and serve vodka from a tray. The story goes that the bear offered a glass of well-chilled vodka to the Tzar who thought the trick so amusing that thereafter Smirnoff was retained to provide for the royal needs. A lucrative coup if ever there was one.

Cucumber wheels

Wash and dry the cucumber. Using a canulating knife, take off strips of skin working along the length of the cucumber, and spacing them evenly apart. This will give a pretty pattern to the outer edge of the cucumber. The canulated pieces of skin may also be used as decoration, either tied into knots or twisted through a highball glass.

When you have finished canulating the cucumber, cut it into fine slices that can be used to decorate the rim of the glass.

Bloody Mary

90ml/3 fl oz vodka
1/4 fresh lime – squeezed
1/4 fresh lemon – squeezed
Dash of Tabasco sauce and Worcestershire sauce
Tomato juice
Ice
Freshly ground pepper and celery salt to taste
Glass: Old fashioned
Garnish: Frost the glass with celery salt. Add a slice of canulated cucumber and a celery stick.

Mix the vodka, lemon juice, lime juice, and sauces together in the frosted glass. Add ice cubes, top off with tomato juice, stir well, and add salt and pepper to taste. Serve with the celery stick.
To make a Virgin Mary, a non-alcoholic version, omit the vodka from this recipe.
Further non-alcoholic beverages can be found on pages 110-123.

Black Russian

(left)
90ml/3 fl oz vodka
30ml/1 fl oz Kahlua coffee liqueur
Ice – cracked
Glass: Highball or tumbler

Fill a glass three-quarters full with cracked ice, and add the vodka and Kahlua.

Bloodshot

30ml/1 fl oz vodka
90ml/3 fl oz condensed beef stock
60ml/2 fl oz tomato juice
Dash of lime juice
Dash of Worcestershire sauce
Dash of chilli sauce
Ground pepper and celery salt to taste
Ice
Glass: Tumbler or highball
Garnish: Two cherry tomatoes with a slice of cucumber

Shake all the ingredients together in a shaker. Pour into a glass half-filled with ice, then garnish.
To make a Bullshot cocktail, use the same ingredients and method, but leave out the tomato juice.

BARMAN'S NOTES

The flavourless, colourless spirit that we most commonly think of as vodka can be made from any natural substance that contains sugar or starch, e.g. potatoes, sugar beet, molasses, wheat, even grapes. Wheat is the most popular ingredient in the west, whereas in Poland and Russia potatoes are sometimes used. One of the great commercial assets of this spirit is that no aging and maturation process is needed. Once the rectified spirit has been purified by filtering it through beds of activated charcoal, it can be drunk on the day it is bottled. (A definite economic bonus to the producer.)
Vodka should always be served well chilled, preferably in iced glasses. When poured into a glass, the spirit should have a slightly oily appearance, and impart this to the glass. Traditionally, vodka was served in small short glasses that were used for a toast and then smashed theatrically into the fireplace or against a wall. Legend has it that Tzar Peter the Great used to sprinkle black pepper on his vodka. Today's Pertsovka vodka was inspired by this – it is dark brown in colour and slightly peppery to taste.

Orange and lemon slice with maraschino cherry and mint

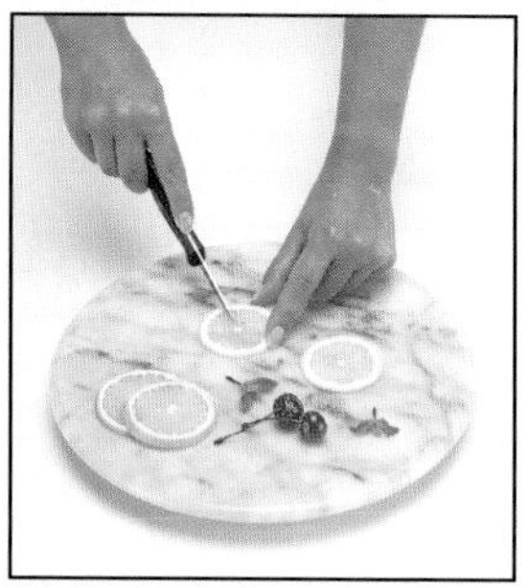

For this garnish you will need an orange, a lemon, a maraschino cherry with its stem still attached and fresh mint sprigs. Make sure the orange is larger than the lemon. Cut a thin slice from both the orange and the lemon, and make a cut into the centre of each.

Take a maraschino cherry. If it has been stoned, there will be a hole in which to place the mint leaves. If not, make a tiny hole with the tip of a sharp knife. Then make a tiny slit in the opposite side of the cherry and place the orange and lemon slice with the cherry over the rim of the glass as a garnish.

Singapore Sling

60ml/2 fl oz gin
30ml/1 fl oz fresh lemon juice
30ml/1 fl oz cherry brandy
Soda water
Ice
Glass: Goblet
Garnish: Slices of orange and lemon, maraschino cherry and a sprig of mint

Pour the ingredients into a glass half-filled with ice. Stir and top off with soda water. Decorate with the garnish.

Martini

90ml/3 fl oz gin
30ml/1 fl oz dry vermouth
Ice
Glass: Martini
Garnish: An olive and a lemon peel twist

Stir the gin, vermouth and ice together in a mixing glass. Strain into the martini glass and garnish.

Bronx Cocktail

60ml/2 fl oz gin
30ml/1 fl oz orange juice
Dash of dry vermouth
Dash of sweet vermouth
Ice – cracked and cubed
Glass: Tall goblet or highball
Garnish: Orange peel twist

Shake all the ingredients together with the cracked ice. Strain into the glass half-filled with cubed ice and garnish.

BARMAN'S NOTES

The choice of gin-based cocktails is so huge that it really has proved difficult to decide on the selection featured in this section. But one that is a must – possibly the most famous cocktail in the world – is the Martini. In this case, the choice is a dry martini – a combination of gin and dry vermouth. The proportions used are the subject of great debate, as indeed are the origins of the cocktail.
Some believe that it was first created by a bartender named Martini working in the Knickerbocker Club in New York in about 1915. Others say that a representative working for the vermouth company Martini and Rossi actually invented the drink. The earliest source for the Martini suggests that it derived from a Martinez cocktail which was included in a bartending book dating from the late 19th century.
The debate over the correct proportions is just as uncertain. The measurements used here give an average Martini, but if you prefer a drier drink, use more gin and less vermouth. However you like it, always stir with ice, strain, and serve garnished with a lemon twist or a green olive. You can even get away with having it on the rocks nowadays.

Tom Collins

60ml/2 fl oz gin
30ml/1 fl oz lemon juice
1 teaspoon caster sugar
Soda water
Ice
Glass: Highball
Garnish: Orange wheel and a maraschino cherry

Pour the gin, lemon juice, and sugar into an ice-filled shaker. Shake, and strain into the serving glass half-filled with ice. Top off with the soda water.

Gimlet

60ml/2 fl oz gin
15ml/½ fl oz lime juice
Ice
Glass: Cocktail
Garnish: A wedge of lime

Pour the gin and lime juice into a mixing glass half-filled with ice and stir well. Strain into the serving glass, and garnish with a wedge of lime.

Strawberry Dawn

60ml/2 fl oz gin
45ml/1½ fl oz coconut cream
4 very ripe strawberries
Ice – crushed
Glass: Goblet
Garnish: A strawberry fan

Mix the gin, coconut cream and strawberries in a blender with plenty of crushed ice (a couple of scoops). Only give the drink a very quick whizz, otherwise it will be too thin. Pour into the goblet, decorate and serve.

Za Za

45ml/1½ fl oz gin
45ml/1½ fl oz red Dubonnet
Dash of Angostura bitters
Glass: Cocktail

Pour a dash of Angostura bitters into the bottom of the glass. Add the gin and Dubonnet, and stir.

Negroni

30ml/1 fl oz gin
30ml/1 fl oz Campari
30ml/1 fl oz sweet vermouth
Soda water (optional)
Ice
Glass: Highball
Garnish: A slice of lime

Pour the gin, Campari and sweet vermouth over ice for the original cocktail. For a longer, lighter drink top off with soda water.

Alexander

30ml/1 fl oz gin
30ml/1 fl oz brown crème de cacao
30ml/1 fl oz fresh cream
Glass: Cocktail
Garnish: Sugar-frosted glass and chocolate shavings

Shake all the ingredients together and pour into the frosted glass. Add the chocolate garnish to the surface of the drink.

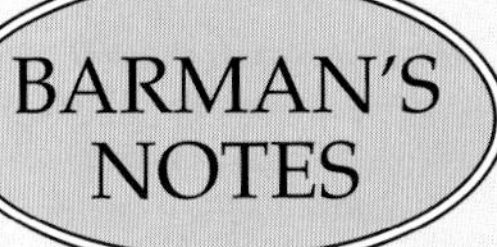

Gin was originally invented for medicinal purposes in the mid-1500s by a Dr. Franciscus de la Boe of the medical school of the University of Leiden in the Netherlands. It was conceived as a cheap, purifying tonic, as both alcohol and juniper berries (used to flavour it) have strong diuretic qualities. The juniper-flavoured spirit was named "genièvre", which means juniper in French. This was rendered as "genever" by the Dutch. It was British troops fighting in Holland in the 17th century who christened the spirit gin. They drank it before going into battle, and the soldiers' drunken bravado became known as Dutch courage.

The gins made in Holland are now divided into two categories – oude jenever (old genever) and jonge jenever (young genever). The names relate to their flavour and style rather than their age. Oude jenever is a stronger, more pungent gin, whereas jonge jenever, which is more popular, has a lighter flavour. Perhaps the most famous gin is London Dry, originally made in London, and now made in distilleries all over the world. A gin that is less dry and more aromatic than London Dry is Plymouth gin. This spirit is very much associated with the British Royal Navy and it takes its name from the naval port of Plymouth.

Lemon rind knot

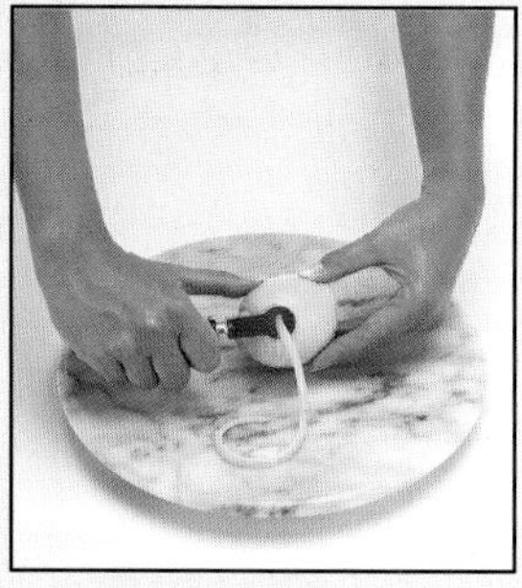

Choose a firm, smooth-skinned lemon if possible. Wash and dry the lemon. With a canulating knife, remove a coil of lemon rind, and scrape off any white pith with the edge of a sharp knife.

Then simply twist the prepared rind into a knot and drop it into the cocktail.

Blue Lady

30ml/1 fl oz gin
60ml/2 fl oz blue Curaçao
30ml/1 fl oz fresh lemon juice
1 teaspoon egg white
Ice
Glass: Cocktail

Shake all the ingredients together with ice, then strain into the glass.

Jet Black

60ml/2 fl oz gin
Dash of sweet vermouth
2 teaspoons black sambuca
Ice
Glass: Cocktail
Garnish: Half a lemon slice and a cocktail cherry

Stir all the ingredients together with ice in a mixing glass. Strain into the serving glass and garnish.

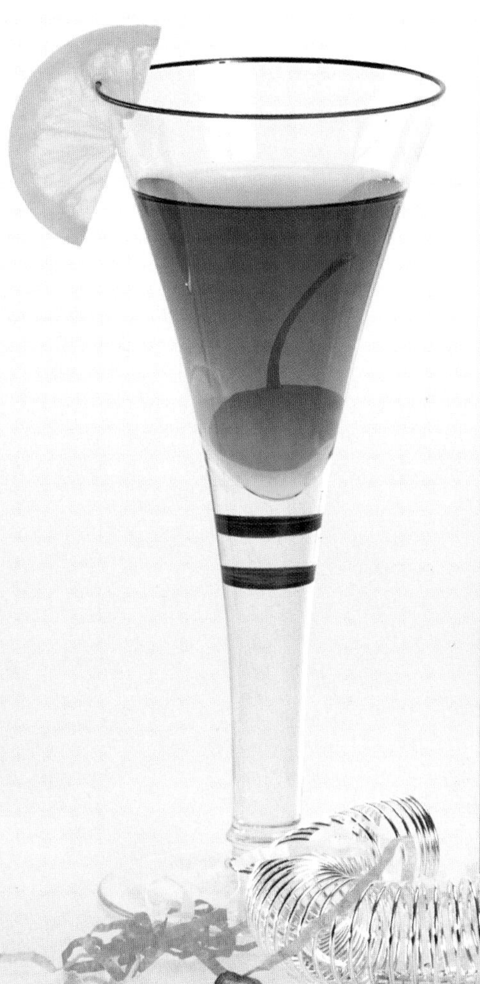

Green Dragon

60ml/2 fl oz gin
30ml/1 fl oz green crème de menthe
15ml/½ fl oz kümmel
15ml/½ fl oz lemon juice
Glass: Cocktail
Garnish: A twist of lemon

Shake all the ingredients together, and pour into a glass half-filled with cracked ice.

Fluffy Duck

60ml/2 fl oz gin
60ml/2 fl oz advocaat (egg-and-brandy cordial)
30ml/1 fl oz Cointreau
30ml/1 fl oz orange juice
Soda water
Ice
Glass: Highball
Garnish: Orange wheel and cherry

Pour the ingredients into an ice-filled glass, stir well and top off with soda water.

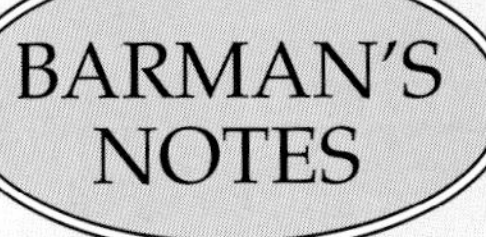

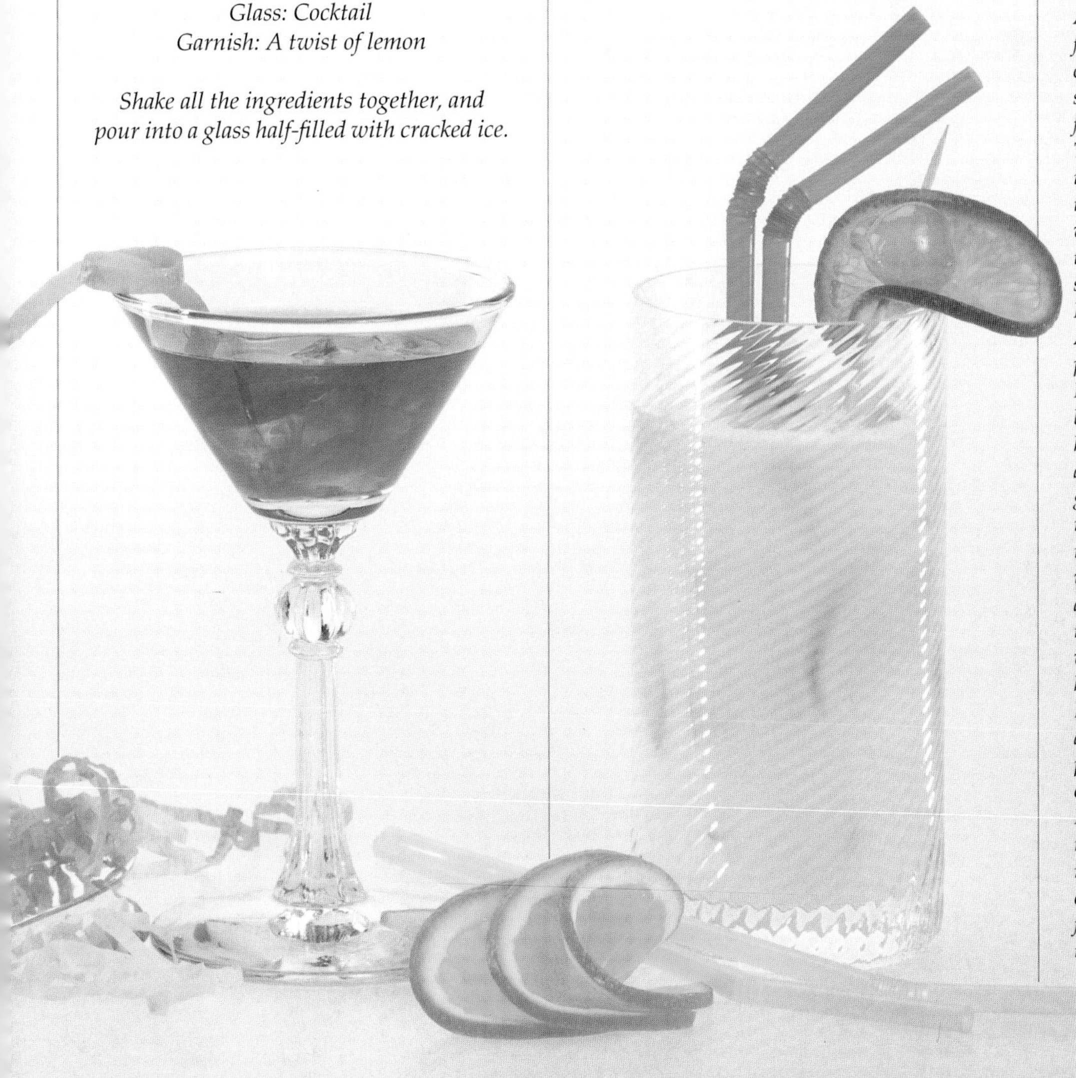

BARMAN'S NOTES

The flavour of gin is predominantly that of juniper berries. The flavouring additives added to gin are called botanicals by the distiller, because most of them are natural plant ingredients. Most American and English gins are distilled from a mash mainly made up of wheat. After the cooked mash has fermented, it is distilled in a continuous still until a very strong, totally neutral, flavourless alcohol is achieved. Then this neutral spirit is put into a pot-still and redistilled to add flavours to it. Distilled water may be added to the gin to reduce its high alcoholic strength before bottling. Flavours popularly added to American gins include pineapple, orange and mint. In the 18th century juniper berries were falsely believed to have the power to induce an abortion, and because of this gin was nicknamed "mothers' ruin" or "ladies' delight". It used to be regarded as a rather vulgar drink. It was widely available and very cheap and the debauched lifestyle of those who overindulged became known as living in "Gin Lane", where the seedy shops advertised "Drunk for one penny, dead drunk for two, clean straw for nothing". Fortunately for the gin makers, attitudes changed radically and in the 20th century gin became the foundation for many traditional cocktails.

Lemon butterfly twist

Choose a thin-skinned lemon. Wash and dry the fruit. Cut a thin lemon slice, and then cut this from the centre to the edge. Push a cocktail stick through the rind about half an inch away from the cut.

Taking hold of the lemon slice on the other side of the cut, twist the lemon back to form a loop in the middle, and tuck the other cut edge into a position so that it aligns with the first. Spear the cocktail stick right through to secure.

Rattlesnake

60ml/2 fl oz blended whisky
15ml/½ fl oz pastis (e.g. Ricard or Pernod)
Juice of 1 lemon
A pinch of icing sugar
1 egg white
Ice
Glass: Cocktail
Garnish: Zest of half an orange

Combine all the ingredients in the shaker, shake well, and strain into the serving glass.

Whisky Sour

60ml/2 fl oz blended whisky
30ml/1 fl oz lemon juice
15ml/½ fl oz gomme syrup (i.e. sugar and water made into a syrup)
Dash of egg white
Glass: Cocktail
Garnish: Lemon loop

Shake all the ingredients together, and pour into the serving glass.

Old Fashioned

90ml/3 fl oz blended whisky
2 dashes of bitters
1 sugar cube or
1 teaspoon caster sugar
Ice
Glass: Old fashioned
Garnish: An orange slice and a cherry

Put the sugar into the glass, add the bitters, and mix together with a spoon. Fill the glass with ice and pour over the whisky. Garnish.

Bourbon Mint Julep

90ml/3 fl oz bourbon
4 or 5 mint leaves
1 teaspoon caster sugar
A few drops of water
Ice – crushed
Glass: Highball
Garnish: A sprig of mint

Lightly muddle together the mint leaves and sugar with a few drops of water in the bottom of the glass. Then almost fill the glass with crushed ice, and pour the bourbon over it. Decorate with a sprig of mint.

BARMAN'S NOTES

The name whisky or whiskey is derived from the Gaelic word "usquebaugh" meaning the "water of life". In the USA and Ireland it is spelt whiskey – with an "e." Scotch whisky can only be produced in Scotland. Other types of whisky are made all over the world. The Scots generally use two types of whisky in the production of blended Scotch: a malt whisky, which gives the blend character and body, and, to add a little lightness, a relatively flavourless grain whisky is added in.
American whiskeys fall into fairly distinct brackets:

- *Blended whiskey, which covers about 47 per cent of the American whiskeys.*
- *Light whiskey, which is made from a very high percentage of corn.*
- *Rye whiskey, which is made from a mash containing barley and at least 51 per cent rye.*
- *Tennessee whiskey, which must be made in Tennessee and contain at least 51 percent of one grain – corn.*
- *Corn whiskey, which must use at least 80 percent corn (maize).*
- *Barley, malt, and rye malt whiskey – all these contain 51 per cent of these grains.*
- *The king of American whiskeys, though, is bourbon – first made in Bourbon County, Kentucky – which must contain at least 51 per cent corn, be bottled at not less than 80° proof, and be matured for at least two years in virgin white oak casks that have been charred inside.*

Single loop lemon knot

Wash and dry the lemon and remove a fairly long continuous piece of lemon rind (approximately 3-4 inches long) with a canulating knife. Remove any pith, then loosely tie a simple knot toward one end of the lemon rind.

Holding the knot in one hand, carefully thread the longer lemon rind "tail" back through the hole in the knot and tighten by pulling as if tying a bow. Then drop it into the cocktail as a garnish on its own or to accompany an olive or cherry.

Dry Manhattan

60ml/2 fl oz rye whiskey
30ml/1 fl oz dry French vermouth
Dash of bitters
Ice
Glass: Cocktail
Garnish: A maraschino cherry and a twist of lemon peel

In a mixing glass, add the whiskey, vermouth, and bitters to the ice, and stir well. Then strain into the serving glass and garnish.
For a regular Manhattan, substitute sweet red vermouth for the dry vermouth, and use three dashes of bitters.

Black Hawk

75ml/2½ fl oz whisky
30ml/1 fl oz sloe gin
Ice
Glass: Old fashioned

Mix the whisky, sloe gin and ice together in a mixing glass. Then strain into the serving glass.

Irish Cocktail

45ml/1½ fl oz Irish whiskey
6 dashes of green crème de menthe
3 dashes of green Chartreuse
Ice
Glass: Cocktail
Garnish: A green and a red cherry

Pour all the ingredients into a shaker, shake, then strain into the serving glass.

Sand Dance

45ml/1½ fl oz blended whisky
30ml/1 fl oz cherry brandy
60ml/2 fl oz cranberry juice
Ice
Glass: Highball
Garnish: A canulated lime peel twist

Fill the glass with ice, pour in all the ingredients, and stir well. You may make the Sand Dance into a longer, lighter drink by adding double the quantity of cranberry juice, and topping off with soda water.

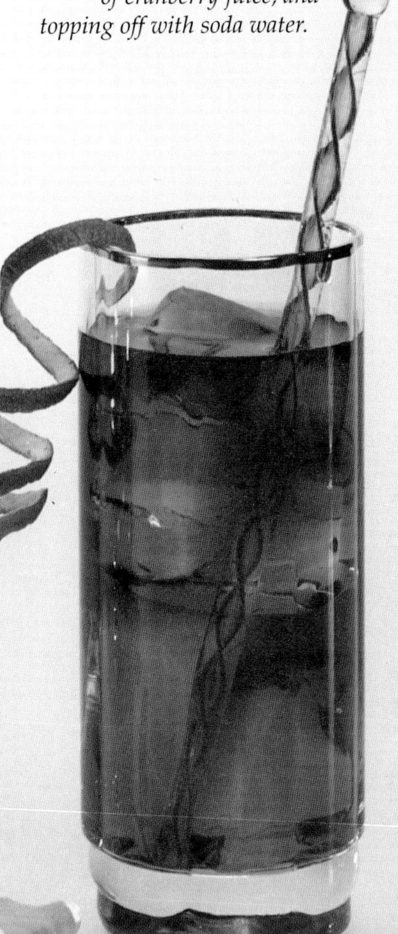

BARMAN'S NOTES

There are numerous cocktails based on American whiskeys, so you are really spoiled for choice. I have selected a few of them, trying to show you some of the variety available within this section.

One old favourite you may also like to try is a Highball, nowadays a term describing any long glass, but originally a specific bourbon-based cocktail using 45ml/1 measure of bourbon poured over ice with ginger ale added to taste. This has now become known as a Seven and Seven, because it frequently uses Seagram's 7 blend topped off with 7-Up. Another drink based on bourbon is Southern Comfort, almost a bottled cocktail in its own right. It has an interesting story attached to it. In the late 19th century a popular cocktail was Cuffs and Buttons. This was a combination of bourbon with peach liqueur, this recipe also being a favourite as a marinade for peaches. The sweet, fruity taste of the peaches seemed to make the bourbon more palatable for those not normally inclined to drink it straight. A bartender in Missouri changed the name of the Cuffs and Buttons to Southern Comfort, and it became so popular that it has been produced in bottled form under this name ever since.

Preparing a pineapple container

Choose a small ripe pineapple and cut about a third of it off the top. With a sharp knife cut around the flesh of the pineapple just inside the skin. Then scoop out all the flesh with a spoon, leaving an ideal drinks container for a number of cocktails. Do not discard the flesh as it can be made into a delicious fruit purée in the blender.

Bahama Mama

15ml/½ fl oz 151°-proof rum
15ml/½ fl oz dark rum
15ml/½ fl oz coconut liqueur
15ml/½ fl oz coffee liqueur
30ml/1 fl oz freshly squeezed lemon juice
125ml/4 fl oz pineapple juice
Ice – cracked
Glass: Highball
Garnish: A coloured cherry, wedge of fresh pineapple and pineapple leaves.

Combine the ingredients in a mixing glass. Pour into a serving glass half-filled with ice and garnish.

Cuba Libre

75ml/2½ fl oz light rum
150ml/5 fl oz cola
Juice of ¼ lemon
Juice of ¼ lime
Ice
Glass: Highball
Garnish: A long lime peel twist and two slices of lemon

Pour the rum and fruit juices into the ice-filled glass, and stir well. Top off with the cola, and then garnish.

Planter's Punch

100ml/3½ fl oz Jamaican rum
30ml/1 fl oz lime juice
30ml/1 fl oz fresh orange juice
30ml/1 fl oz pineapple juice
Dash of grenadine
Dash of bitters
Soda water
Ice
Glass: A small scooped-out pineapple or a large glass
Garnish: A pineapple wedge, pineapple leaves, an orange and a lime slice, and cherries. Serve with straws.

Pour the rum, fruit juices, bitters, grenadine and ice into a shaker, shake, and strain into the pineapple half-filled with ice cubes. Top off with soda water to taste and garnish.

Blue Heaven

45ml/1½ fl oz white rum
15ml/½ fl oz amaretto
15ml/½ fl oz blue Curaçao
15ml/½ fl oz fresh lime juice
90-100ml/3-3½ fl oz pineapple juice
Ice
Glass: Highball or stemmed goblet
Garnish: Pineapple leaves, a lime slice and a coloured cherry

Pour all the ingredients into a shaker, shake, but do not strain. Then pour into the serving glass and garnish.

Zombie

60ml/2 fl oz white rum
60ml/2 fl oz golden rum
60ml/2 fl oz dark rum
30ml/1 fl oz apricot liqueur
30ml/1 fl oz pineapple juice
30ml/1 fl oz lime juice
A dash of gomme syrup (sugar and water mix)
Ice – cracked
Glass: Highball
Garnish: A wedge of pineapple, orange, lemon, and lime slices.

Half-fill the glass with ice, add all the ingredients, and stir well.

BARMAN'S NOTES

A spirit distilled from sugar cane, rum was first made in the West Indies in the 16th century by Spanish settlers who worked in the sugar factories there. They noticed that once the sugar had been extracted from the sugar cane, they were left with sticky molasses as a by-product, and this naturally fermented in the heat. They then distilled the fermented molasses and were left with a strong dark spirit – rum.

Rum has enjoyed something of a chequered history. It has been used medicinally, and was freely distributed as part of George Washington's electoral campaign. However, the fact that it helped the horrific slave trade to continue adds a darker note. The slaves for the sugar cane fields were often African natives transported to the Caribbean in British ships. They were traded there for raw molasses which was shipped to the American colonies to be made into rum. This rum would then be used to exchange for more African slaves, and so the notorious "Triangle Trade" continued.

Rum even played its part in the American Revolution, as the famous Boston Tea Party of 1773 was a revolt aimed against the taxes imposed on tea and molasses by the British government. It was the rum-running ships heading for the New England states that broke the British naval blockade in the Revolutionary War.

Preparing coconut slices

When choosing a coconut make sure that it feels heavy, and that when shaken you can hear that it holds plenty of milk. Pierce two holes in the top of the coconut, drain the milk, then bake it in a moderate oven for about 15 minutes. This makes the flesh shrink away from the shell, making it easier to remove the flesh in large pieces. Crack the shell when cool, and ease away a portion of flesh with the edge of a knife.

Hold the coconut flesh securely and cut long slices of it to use as decoration. You may leave the dark inner skin on to make a more attractive contrast in the garnish, or it may be removed.

Virgin Strawberry Daiquiri

125ml/4 fl oz fresh strawberry juice or
225g/8 oz strawberries puréed and sieved
150ml/5 fl oz freshly squeezed orange juice
Dash of lime juice
Dash of lemon juice
Ice – 480ml/16 fl oz cracked
Glass: Daiquiri glass
Garnish: A strawberry slice decorated with strawberry leaves

Put all the fruit juices with half the ice into the blender, and blend very quickly on high. Then pour into the serving glass filled with the other cup of ice, and garnish.

Surrey Slider

60ml/2 fl oz golden rum
30ml/1 fl oz peach schnapps
90ml/3 fl oz orange juice
Ice
Glass: Highball
Garnish: An orange slice

Almost fill the glass with ice, and then pour in all the ingredients. Stir well, then garnish.

Piña Colada

90ml/3 fl oz white rum
125ml/4 fl oz pineapple juice
60ml/2 fl oz coconut cream
Ice – crushed, approx. 300ml/10 fl oz
Glass: Serve in a small, scooped-out coconut shell, or, if unobtainable, a highball glass
Garnish: Pineapple wedges, a red cherry, and coconut slices

Pour all the ingredients into a blender, and blend well at high speed. Then pour into the prepared coconut shell.

Yellow Bird

90ml/3 fl oz white rum
30ml/1 fl oz Galliano
30ml/1 fl oz orange liqueur
30ml/1 fl oz fresh lime juice
Ice
Glass: Champagne tulip
Garnish: A lime slice

Pour all the ingredients into a shaker, shake, then pour into the serving glass.

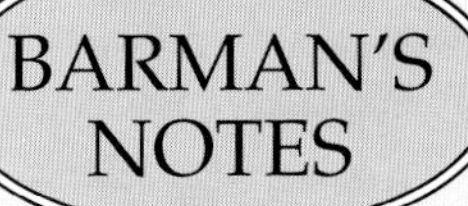

Various types of rums are produced around the world. Probably the best known is Jamaica rum – the dark, heavier style of rum is most associated with this island. Jamaica produces some of the finest and strongest, one being available at a breathtaking 151° proof! Other types include Cuban light rums – Cuba was the original home of the famous Bacardi brand. The light rum distillers usually offer a gold anejo (aged) rum variety as well. Guyana, Trinidad, Barbados, Martinique and Guadeloupe, Haiti and Puerto Rico are all famous for their rums.
Rum is also distilled outside the Caribbean. For instance, Batavia arak is made in Java and bottled in Holland. South America and Australia also produce it.
Planter's Punch (see page 56) is one of the oldest recipes using rum, dating back to the 17th century. An old rhyme summarizes the recipe:
"One of sour, (lime juice)
Two of sweet, (sugar syrup)
Three of strong, (rum)
Four of weak (ice)"
Taken literally it makes a pretty strong drink!
A more modern and very popular drink using rum is a Daiquiri, which can be made by shaking together with ice 135ml/4½ fl oz of white rum, 45ml/1½ fl oz of lemon or lime juice and 1 teaspoon of caster sugar. Strain this into a cocktail glass.

Green and red apple chevrons

Choose a red apple and a green apple that match in shape and size as closely as possible. Wash and dry them. Cut two quarters from each colour and, to prevent discoloration, douse the flesh with lemon juice. With a sharp knife cut a wedge from the skin side of the apple, then cut a smaller one from the original segment. You may keep it simple with just two incisions, or continue with as many as four or five cuts in one quarter. Repeat this process with the other apple. To put the chevron together, alternate one green and one red wedge until the chevron is completed. Either attach it to the glass with a cocktail stick, or make a smaller slit in the flesh and hook it over the rim of the glass.

April Shower

45ml/1½ fl oz brandy
30ml/1 fl oz Bénédictine
60ml/2 fl oz orange juice
Soda water
Ice
Glass: Wine goblet
Garnish: Kumquat and cucumber swirl

Half-fill the glass with ice, add the brandy, Bénédictine, and orange juice. Stir, then top off with the soda water.

Apple Jack Light

60ml/2 fl oz brandy
175ml/6 fl oz apple juice
Ice
Glass: Highball
Garnish: Two-tone apple chevron

Half-fill the glass with ice. Pour over the brandy, and top off with the apple juice. Stir.

T.N.T.

60ml/2 fl oz brandy
30ml/1 fl oz orange Curaçao
Dash of pastis
Dash of bitters
Glass: Cocktail

Stir all the ingredients together in the serving glass.

Apple Jack

60ml/2 fl oz brandy
30ml/1 fl oz Calvados
30ml/1 fl oz Poire William (pear liqueur)
30ml/1 fl oz grenadine
30ml/1 fl oz lemon juice
Ice
Glass: Old fashioned
Garnish: Apple slice

Pour everything into a shaker and shake well. Strain into the serving glass half-filled with ice.

BARMAN'S NOTES

Strictly speaking, any fruit that is fermented and then distilled produces a spirit called brandy.
However, most spirits referred to as brandy nowadays are distilled from grape wine. Others can be made from various mashes such as apricots, apples, cherries or plums. Liqueurs and cordials, still very popular in their own right, are made in a different way. Fruit is infused or macerated in a ready-made spirit base, and the resulting drink is often sweetened.
In both Italy and Spain, a brandy-type spirit made from wine was produced as early as the 13th century. It took over a 100 years for the French to take up the cause.
Now, however, France definitely leads the world in the production of brandy. The king of brandy, cognac, is named after an ancient city in south-west France. Not any brandy can be called cognac; only those distilled from the grapes grown in the Charente vineyards of this famous region are allowed to bear the name. The industry is controlled by strict regulations just as the best French wine production is. All cognac must be aged for at least two years in oak barrels. Armagnac, lying south of Cognac, is also very famous for its fine brandy.

Cherry, orange and pineapple garnish

For a single garnish take two pineapple leaves, a wedge from a slice of pineapple, half a slice of orange and a cherry. You will need a cocktail stick or sword to keep everything in position.

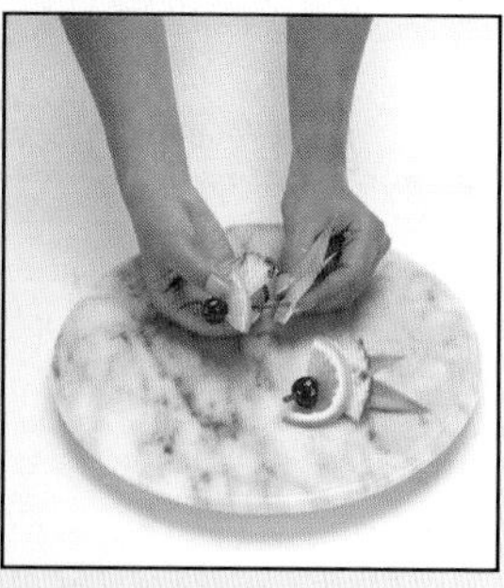

First thread the cherry onto the cocktail stick or sword. Follow this with the orange slice, the wedge of pineapple and finally the two pineapple leaves. Balance the garnish across the rim of the glass, and separate the pineapple leaves into a V shape.

Mint Royal

45ml/1½ fl oz brandy
45ml/1½ fl oz mint chocolate liqueur
45ml/1½ fl oz lemon juice
1 egg white
Ice
Glass: Cocktail
Garnish: Half a lemon slice and a sprig of mint

Pour all the ingredients into the shaker, shake, and strain into the serving glass.

Red Hackle

45ml/1½ fl oz brandy
30ml/1 fl oz red Dubonnet
15ml/½ fl oz grenadine
Ice
Glass: Cocktail
Garnish: A cocktail cherry

Shake all the ingredients together with one cube of ice, then strain into the serving glass.

Moulin Rouge

60ml/2 fl oz brandy
90ml/3 fl oz fresh pineapple juice
Sparkling white wine – well chilled
Ice
Glass: Highball
Garnish: A wedge of pineapple, pineapple leaves, half a slice of orange and a cherry.

Half-fill the glass with ice, pour over the brandy and pineapple juice, and top off with the chilled wine. For a lighter, less alcoholic version, use sparkling mineral water instead of sparkling white wine.

Brandy Alexander

45ml/1½ fl oz brandy
45ml/1½ fl oz fresh cream
30ml/1 fl oz white crème de cacao
Ice
Glass: Champagne saucer
Garnish: Freshly grated nutmeg

Pour all the ingredients into a shaker, shake, and strain into the serving glass. Then dust with freshly grated nutmeg.

BARMAN'S NOTES

The colour of a brandy is not always a sure guide to its quality, but its aroma is! One way of checking quality is, when you have finished your glass of brandy, take a dry cloth and wipe the glass clean. Take a sniff from the cloth. If it smells of vanilla, the brandy was young and possibly raw. If it has a delicate woody smell, it is a well-aged spirit. Also look at your glass just as you finish drinking and watch to see if the spirit clings to the glass or if it just slides off. The latter characteristic may mean the addition of sweetenings or caramel flavours, meaning a poorer quality brandy. One fairly certain way of evaluating a brandy is by how much it costs! The more expensive it is, generally the older and better it is, as the old cask-aged brandies cost a lot more than the young ones. A brandy should be served in a glass that is not too big for the hands to hold easily. The heat from your cupped palms alone should warm the brandy to its correct temperature as you swirl it slowly in the glass. Traditionally it is served in a balloon-shaped glass, although the French prefer a tulip-shaped goblet as they believe that it allows you to appreciate the bouquet more. The really huge balloon glasses and the practice of heating brandy over a flame are not to be recommended.

Orange spiral

Choose a smooth-skinned orange. Wash and dry it. Canulate it in one continuous piece around one third of the orange. Cut off the portion that you have canulated, taking care not to nip off the long coil of rind. Then remove the slice of orange with the coil of rind attached. Cut into the centre of the slice of orange next to where the coil is attached, then cut a quarter section from this. Carefully make a tiny slit in the rind of the orange segment by the coil and slip this over the rim of the glass. Coil the orange rind around the outside of the glass right down to the base. This may also be done with a lime, lemon, or even a grapefruit as an alternative.

Mimosa

125ml/4 fl oz chilled champagne
45ml/1½ fl oz fresh orange juice
15ml/½ fl oz orange Curaçao
Glass: Champagne flute
Garnish: Orange spiral

Pour the Curaçao and the fresh orange juice into the glass, and top off with the champagne.
For a Buck's Fizz, use equal proportions of champagne and orange juice together.

Champagne Cocktail

Chilled champagne
30ml/1 fl oz brandy
One sugar lump
Approx 6 drops of Angostura bitters
Glass: Champagne flute

Put the sugar lump in the bottom of the glass and add enough bitters to soak into the sugar. Add the brandy and top off with the champagne.

Death in the Afternoon

175ml/5 fl oz well chilled champagne
30ml/1 fl oz pastis
Glass: Champagne flute

Pour the pastis into the glass and top off with the champagne.

Champagne Charlie

130ml/4½ fl oz chilled champagne
45ml/1 measure apricot brandy
Glass: Champagne flute

Pour the apricot brandy into the glass and top off with the champagne.

BARMAN'S NOTES

Champagne is a wine of distinction, rising to any occasion. There are various styles available on the market, but, to bear the name champagne, they all have to be produced from grapes grown in a particular area in northern France, around the valley of the River Marne and the towns of Reims, Epernay and Ay, and to have been produced by the champagne method in which a secondary fermentation takes place in the bottle. It is this process that gives champagne its fizz. The champagne producers guard their exclusive name jealously. In 1993, they went to court to prevent the Yves St. Laurent company from using the word "Champagne" as a name of a perfume. Champagne is a very labour-intensive product to produce and in the past this was reflected in its price. Nowadays, more reasonably priced and still very palatable champagnes may be purchased. And, of course, sparkling wines from other countries, notably Spain, Australia, the United States and Germany, offer excellent value and quality if an alternative is required. These are quite acceptable when making cocktails that include other highly flavoured ingredients, as the delicate flavour of French champagne can easily be masked by other ingredients.

Strawberry fan

Choose a firm, nicely shaped strawberry with the leaves still attached. Wash and dry the fruit then, with a very sharp knife, slice vertically through the fruit from just below its top to the bottom, being careful not to cut right through a slice or to cut the leaves off. Make about five cuts in this way.

To fan the fruit, lie it on the work surface and gently spread apart the slices into a fan. This garnish can be slipped over the rim of the glass, or can hang over the rim, speared by a cocktail stick.

Kir Royal

150ml/5 fl oz chilled champagne
30ml/1 fl oz cassis
Glass: Champagne flute
Garnish: A strawberry fan or a small string of blackcurrants.

Pour the cassis into the glass, and top off with the champagne.

Green Bubbles

(left)
150ml/5 fl oz chilled champagne
30ml/1 fl oz Midori melon liqueur
30ml/1 fl oz Poire William liqueur
Glass: Champagne flute

Mix the Midori and Poire William together in the glass, and top off with the champagne.

Blue Bird

140ml/4½ fl oz chilled champagne
45ml/1 measure blue Curaçao
Glass: Champagne flute

Pour the blue Curaçao into the glass, and top off with the champagne.

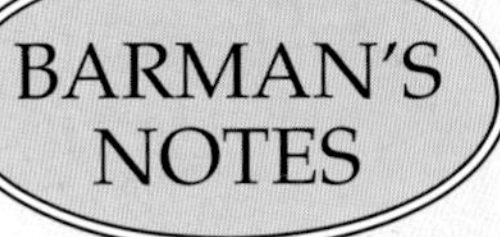

Champagne rosé – pink champagne – is a special type of champagne. It is obtained either by blending some of the region's red wine with the white in the production, or by allowing the skins of the Pinot Noir black grapes to remain in the vat long enough to slightly tint the wine. This method allows the wine to be made entirely from black grapes – the French call it "Rosé de. Noirs".

Champagne needs to be served nicely chilled at about 45°F/ 7°C. If it is too cold, it will lose its taste. It will not retain its sparkle if served too warm. The best way to chill it is in an ice bucket containing a mixture of ice and water. It will take at least half an hour to cool. Serve in polished, dry champagne flutes or tulip-shaped glasses, which have the best shape to retain the sparkle and bouquet of the wine. Flat champagne saucers, though once popular, are not the ideal shape for a sparkling wine.

To open the bottle safely, first release the wire covering the cork. Hold the neck of the bottle and the cork with a clean dry cloth and twist the bottle very gently, keeping pressure and control on the cork the whole time. Gently ease it from the bottle in this way. It should emerge with a gentle sigh rather than an earth-shattering pop, which could prove very dangerous if the cork is allowed to fly.

Puréeing peaches

Choose ripe, unbruised peaches if using fresh fruit. Remove the skin, halve them, and stone them. Alternatively, you may simply use canned peach halves. Put the fruit into a nylon sieve over a bowl.

With the back of a spoon, slowly press the fruit through the sieve into the bowl, occasionally scraping the fruit from the underside of the sieve, until the required amount of peach purée has been made.

Jim Jams Zizz

45ml/1½ fl oz calvados
45ml/1½ fl oz brandy or brandymel
45ml/1½ fl oz apricot brandy
45ml/1½ fl oz fresh cream
Glass: Heatproof glass
Garnish: A sprinkle of freshly grated nutmeg.

Heat the calvados, brandy and apricot brandy together slowly until warm. Do not boil. Pour into the serving glass, and either float the cream on the top, or mix in the cream as wished. Then sprinkle with the nutmeg.

Peach Comfort

60ml/2 fl oz Southern Comfort
30ml/1 fl oz peach schnapps
60ml/2 fl oz fresh peach juice
Glass: Irish coffee glass

Gently heat all the ingredients until warm. Then pour into the serving glass.

Honeyed Apples

60ml/2 fl oz calvados
1 teaspoon of honey
Hot water
Glass: Heatproof glass

Mix the honey and the calvados in a glass, and top off with hot water.

BARMAN'S NOTES

A hot toddy is usually a drink made up of a spirit of your choice mixed with hot water, lemon, sugar and spices. The warmers referred to here are anything warm and warming. Definitely drinks to keep winter at bay.

The Victorians in England chose to drink their toddies hot and they were generally taken to cure chills and calm and soothe the nerves. Purely medicinal I'm sure! The warmers are nice taken as an after-dinner, pre-bedtime drink. Here is an additional recipe for such an occasion.

Hot Buttered Rum

90ml/3 fl oz dark rum
1 teaspoon of brown sugar
10g/¼ oz pat of butter
Boiling water
Glass: A heat-resistant handled glass
Garnish: Freshly grated nutmeg

Place the sugar in the bottom of the glass, and pour over the boiling water so that the glass is about two-thirds full. Stir to dissolve the sugar, add the butter and the rum, and stir again to mix the ingredients thoroughly. Garnish and serve warm.

Elixir végétal on sugar cubes

Elixir Végétal comes complete with its own wooden case. This little bottle contains a spirit of 140° proof. A good way of taking such a strong drink is on a soaked sugar cube.

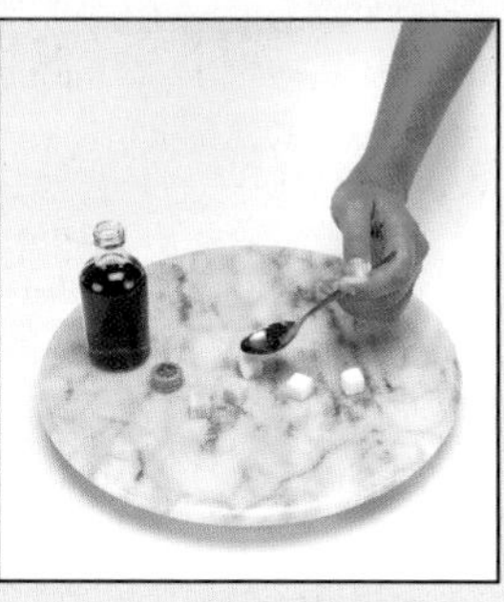

The easiest and least wasteful way of soaking the cube is to put the Elixir Végétal into a teaspoon and then pour it over the sugar cube. Consume immediately.

The Morning After

60ml/2 fl oz brandy
2 dashes bitter herbal digestif
60ml/2 fl oz cream
30ml/1 fl oz milk
1 egg yolk
Ice
Glass: Brandy glass

Pour all the ingredients into a shaker, shake and strain into the serving glass, which should be half-filled with ice.

Elixir Végétal

Elixir Végétal de la Grande-Chartreuse
Glass: Liqueur glass

A small amount may be taken as a digestif, either straight, or on a sugar lump.

Tummy Soother

60ml/2 fl oz brandy
15ml/½ fl oz kümmel
Dash of bitters
Dash of bitter herbal digestif
A small pinch of ground caraway seed
Ice
Glass: Brandy glass

Pour all the ingredients into a shaker, shake, and strain into the serving glass.

Cold Chaser

45ml/1½ fl oz elderflower cordial
Hot water
Glass: Highball
Garnish: A slice of lemon

Pour the elderflower cordial into the serving glass and top off with hot water. Serve with a lemon slice floating on top.

BARMAN'S NOTES

A selection of more unusual pick-me-ups has been chosen for this section. The term pick-me-up (by definition) is a drink, often alcoholic, taken as a stimulant or restorative.

The cold chaser is meant to have beneficial effects for those suffering from a cold or flu. It can be taken hot or cold, the combination of elderflower and lemons being a very traditional remedy.

Elixir végétal, a 140° liqueur classified as a pharmaceutical product, may be taken in very small doses to relieve the common cold. Its herbal ingredients are said to give the liqueur the property of restoring health and prolonging life. An acquired taste for life possibly!

If a non-alcoholic remedy for a queasy stomach is needed, try adding a pinch of bicarbonate of soda to the juice of a lemon in a glass and topping off with boiled water. Sweeten to taste.

Other well-known pick-me-ups include the Prairie Oyster, which is made by putting a barspoon of Worcestershire sauce and tomato sauce into a wine glass with an unbroken egg yolk, two dashes of vinegar, and a dash of pepper. The concoction should be swallowed in one gulp! A Prairie Hen is a similar recipe including the whole egg, and Tabasco sauce instead of tomato sauce.

Kumquat lily flowers

Choose thin-skinned, evenly shaped fruit. Wash and dry them. With a very sharp knife cut along the length of the kumquat from top to bottom, making sure you cut only through the skin and not the flesh. Cut five more times, making six sections in total. Then, with the blade of the knife, carefully peel away the "petals" from the fruit, spreading them out to make lily-like flowers. These can be floated on slices of fruit in the punch or may simply be attached to the rim of a glass for a very attractive garnish.

T's Special

Serves 6-8

375ml/12 fl oz vodka
125ml/4 fl oz white rum
125ml/4 fl oz Cointreau
2 dashes of orange bitters
250ml/8 fl oz bitter lemon
750ml/24 fl oz freshly squeezed orange juice
Ice
Glass: A 2-quart punch bowl, 6-8 highball glasses
Garnish: Lemon and clementine slices with kumquat flowers

Put plenty of ice into the punch bowl, then add the rest of the ingredients and stir. Float the lemon and clementine slices on the top, and balance the kumquat flowers on these like water lilies!

Cool Green Haze

(right)

Serves 6

1 (750 ml.) bottle champagne or dry sparkling white wine
750ml/24 fl oz of lemon-lime soda
75ml/2½ fl oz Midori melon liqueur
75ml/2½ fl oz kiwi fruit liqueur
Ice
Glass: A 5 pint/3 litre pitcher, 6 champagne flutes
Garnish: 3 kiwi fruits, skinned and sliced, 1 pink balled melon, lemon and lime peel twists and knots

Put all the ingredients into the pitcher with plenty of ice. Stir well once, and decorate with the prepared fruit and peel twists.

BARMAN'S NOTES

Punches were introduced into England in the 17th century, after the British captured the island of Jamaica from Spain, when rum was favoured as the spirit mixer. In the 18th and 19th centuries, punches were frequently drunk as an accompaniment to a meal, rather like mineral water is today; hence the large, ornate punchbowls that were prominently featured on the table as centrepieces.
Punch was traditionally a drink made from wine or spirits, such as brandy or rum, into which were mixed sugar, spices, lemons and water. How it got its name is not certain, but it possibly derived from the word "puncheon", a large wine cask holding between 70 and 120 gallons. Another suggestion is that it comes from the Hindi word panch, *meaning five, as more than five ingredients are usually present when making a punch. Punches seem to have lost their popularity over the last few years, which really is a shame. They are underestimated as they can make life so much easier for any host or hostess. Taking the strain out of entertaining any number of guests, they leave time for you to talk to your friends.*

Lemon peel bow

Choose a well-rounded, thin, smooth-skinned lemon for this garnish. Wash and dry the fruit. With a canulating knife, peel off the whole lemon peel in one continuous strip, then remove any white pith from the skin by scraping it with the knife blade.

Now simply tie a large bow with nice long tails with the prepared rind, and attach it to the edge of the glass with a cocktail stick, or float it in the centre of the punch bowl as a pretty garnish.

Summer Sensation!

Serves 4-6

125ml/4 fl oz elderflower cordial
125ml/4 fl oz Rose's lime juice
250ml/8 fl oz sparkling mineral water
500ml/16 fl oz sparkling apple juice
Ice cubes, ideally lime-flavoured
Glass: A 1½ litre/3 pint glass jug, 4-6 highball glasses

Garnish: 1 lemon bow, 1 lime and 1 apple both sliced. Elderflowers when available

Quarter-fill the glass jug with ice, then pour in the rest of the ingredients. Stir and finally add the fruit and flowers. The result is a refreshing summer drink!

Rashbrooke's Rum Punch

Serves 6

1 (750 ml.) bottle medium-light white rum
150ml/5 fl oz Rose's lime juice
225g/8 oz granulated sugar
500ml/16 fl oz water
2 pinches of freshly grated nutmeg
2 dashes of Angostura bitters
Ice
Glass: A 2-3 litre/2½ pint punch bowl, 6 tumblers or old fashioned glasses
Garnish: Lemon and lime slices and peel twists.

Put the sugar and water into a pan and very slowly heat to boiling, stirring constantly. Making sure that the sugar has dissolved completely, simmer for ten minutes. Remove from the heat and allow to cool. Then mix this sugar syrup with the rum and lime juice in the punch bowl with plenty of ice. Add nutmeg and bitters to taste, and garnish.
Deceptively easy to drink; check leg control before standing!

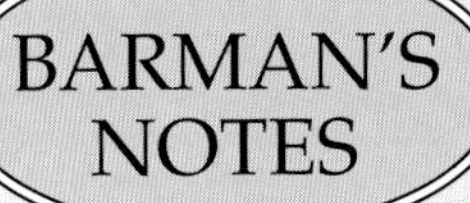

It is customary to serve ice-chilled punches on warm summer days. They make entertaining guests much simpler, as they can be made in advance. If any of the ingredients are fizzy, such as champagne, sparkling wines, soft drinks, cola, or soda water, they should be added at the last minute to keep their effervescence. So should any ice, especially ice cubes, as they tend to melt and so dilute the punch. The last guests to arrive could end up with a very watery drink if you add ice too soon!
The serving bowl can be kept cool by standing it in a larger bowl filled with cracked ice. If you want to add ice to the punch itself, do not add until about 15 minutes before serving, and then add large blocks of ice rather than small cubes. These can be made simply by taking the dividers out of your metal ice trays, or freezing water (perhaps even flavoured water) in cleaned juice cartons. To make the blocks look a little more attractive, slightly colour the water with a vegetable dye that will complement the punch. Alternatively, freeze slices of fruit or flower petals in the ice blocks. They add that extra "something" to a summer drink.

Mango and strawberry slices

Choose unbruised, ripe, but firm fruit. Wash and dry them. Remove the leaves and slice the strawberries lengthways. To make a mango wedge, hold the mango on its side and cut about a third off. The mango has a rather large stone so it cannot be cut in half like other fruit.

Now cut the mango third into wedged slices, and make a small angled slit near the top of the slice through the flesh towards the skin. Also make a slit in the strawberry slice at the leafy end. Then hang the slit fruit over the rim of the glass as garnish.

A Pitcher of Smooth Cider

Serves 4

1 litre/32 fl oz dry sparkling cider
60ml/2 fl oz calvados
60ml/2 fl oz amaretto
60ml/2 fl oz Cointreau
Ice
Glass: A 2-litre/2½-pint jug or pitcher, 4 tumblers
Garnish: 1 segmented orange, 2 sliced apples, 4 sprigs of apple mint, long orange peel twists

Fill about one third of the pitcher with ice. Pour in the liqueurs, mix and top off with the cider. Add the prepared fruit and peel. Serve into the glasses, adding a sprig of mint to each.

Grape and Cranberry Punch

(below right)
Serves 8-10

1 litre/32 fl oz cranberry juice
1 litre/32 fl oz red grape juice
500ml/16 fl oz fresh orange juice
500ml/16 fl oz soda water
125ml/4 fl oz strawberry syrup
Ice
Glass: A 3½-litre/6½-pint pitcher, 8-10 goblets
Garnish: Halved strawberries, seedless red grapes, orange slices

Fill a third of the punchbowl with ice. Add all the ingredients and stir well. Leave to chill for ten minutes before adding slices of peeled orange and the other fruit.

Fruity Maple Punch

Serves 8

750ml bottle of chilled light white wine
750ml/24 fl oz freshly squeezed orange juice
125ml/4 fl oz maple syrup
3 dashes of grenadine
125ml/4 fl oz walnut liqueur – optional
100g/4 oz pecan halves
Plenty of seasonal fresh fruit - chopped - for example, strawberries, raspberries, oranges, melon, peaches
Ice
Glass: Glass punchbowl with 8 highball glasses
Garnish: A selection of chopped and sliced seasonal fruit

Mix the maple syrup, wine and orange juice together in the punchbowl. Pour in 3 dashes of grenadine (and walnut liqueur if using), then all the prepared fruit and nuts. Add plenty of ice about fifteen minutes before serving. Serve chilled.

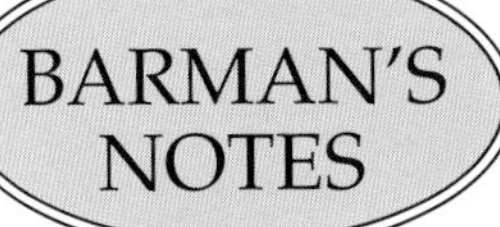

When serving these punches, it is nice to keep the bowl and glasses chilled. For small quantities of punch, the bowl looks pretty standing in a decorative ice bowl. You can always rest the serving glasses in this as well. It will make an attractive centrepiece to any party table.
It is very simple to make. You need two bowls, one for the serving punch bowl and one larger bowl for it to stand in. (Make sure the bowls are made of toughened glass so that they will not crack in the freezer). Pour some water into the larger bowl, then place the smaller bowl in it, and add more water. In the space between the two bowls arrange pieces of fruit, flowers, and leaves in a decorative pattern against the outer bowl. Put into the freezer and freeze until the water is solid. To remove, just before it is needed pour a little warm water into the smaller bowl. This melts the ice sufficiently to allow you to remove the serving bowl. Then stand the larger bowl in lukewarm water just long enough to be able to slip the ice bowl off its mold. Stand it on a lipped tray surrounded by fresh leaves and flowers with either the punchbowl or the glasses keeping cool in it. You will see an example pictured on page 16 of this book.

Banana slices on a sword

Choose a firm, unblemished banana. Peel and slice it into half-inch slices. Cover the slices with lemon juice to prevent discoloration. Thread the slices onto the cocktail stick, spacing them evenly.

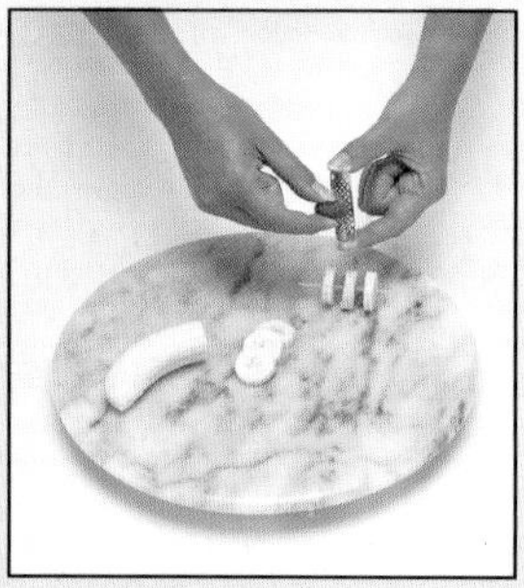

To finish the garnish, cover with a dusting of freshly grated nutmeg.

Autumn Pudding Punch

Serves 6-8

750ml/24 fl oz bottle of plum wine or any other fruit wine
500-750ml/16-24 fl oz blackberry-flavoured mineral water or soda water
90ml/3 fl oz crème de cassis
90ml/3 fl oz crème de framboise
90ml/3 fl oz Poire William liqueur
Ice
Glass: A 2½ pint/2-3 litre punch bowl, 8 stemmed wine goblets

Garnish: A selection of fresh fruits, such as blackcurrants, raspberries, pears and plums

Mix all the ingredients, except the ice, together in a punchbowl. Allow to stand for at least fifteen minutes for the flavours to blend. Add the ice and fruits and serve, giving everyone a good selection of fruit in their glass.

Hot Banana Punch

Serves 8

2 ripe bananas
500ml/6 fl oz coconut milk
250ml/8 fl oz coconut cream
250ml/8 fl oz fresh milk
125ml/4 fl oz crème de bananes liqueur
60ml/2 fl oz golden rum
Glass: A 2 litre/3 pint heatproof punchbowl, 8 goblets
Garnish: 3 slices of banana on a cocktail stick sprinkled with nutmeg. If you have time, it looks attractive to serve the punch in glasses frosted with yellow-tinted coconut

Roughly slice the bananas and put them with the rest of the ingredients into a blender. Blend quickly on high. Transfer the mixture into a pan and heat very slowly over a low flame. Do not boil; serve warm. It is equally nice served cold!

BARMAN'S NOTES

For the Autumn Pudding Punch in this section I have tried to create the feeling of those slightly cooler autumn days, when we can enjoy the last of the late summer fruits, which also remind us that it will not be long until those cold winter months and dark evenings are upon us. To make this a less alcoholic punch, try using red grape juice in place of the fruit wine. It is the fresh fruits soaking in the punch that give it the feel of autumn, and they are great to eat with ice-cream, or on their own, once the alcohol has been consumed.
When the colder months of winter arrive, there is nothing more welcoming than being offered a glass of hot punch. It really surprises me that punches are not made more often; you do not have to be celebrating or entertaining to drink them. Reduce the quantities for smaller numbers, or just make enough for a couple of glasses.
A lot of drinks that would normally be drunk cold can be adapted to a warmed version. Any of the freshly squeezed juices can be heated, so making very healthy drinks and punches. Warmed cranberry juice is delicious and even mango nectar and apricot juice diluted slightly with hot water are extremely tasty. Try making the cranberry and grape recipe from the summer punch section or even Summer Sensation and warming them.

Hot Apple Pie Punch

Serves 4-6

1 litre/32 fl oz dry cider
125ml/4 fl oz calvados
125ml/4 fl oz dark rum
125g/4 oz sultanas
4 x 5cm/2-inch pieces of cinnamon stick
16 cloves
1 apple, cored, halved and sliced
Glass: A 2 litre/3½ pint heatproof jug or punchbowl, 4-6 heatproof glasses

Put the sultanas into a bowl with the rum and allow to soak for two hours. Then mix in all the other ingredients. Pour into a pan and heat very slowly; do not allow to boil. Serve hot with the sultanas and a cinnamon stick in each glass and the cloves and apple slices floating in the mixture. Serve straight, or mix in some fresh cream if you want to achieve that real homemade apple pie taste.

Coring an apple

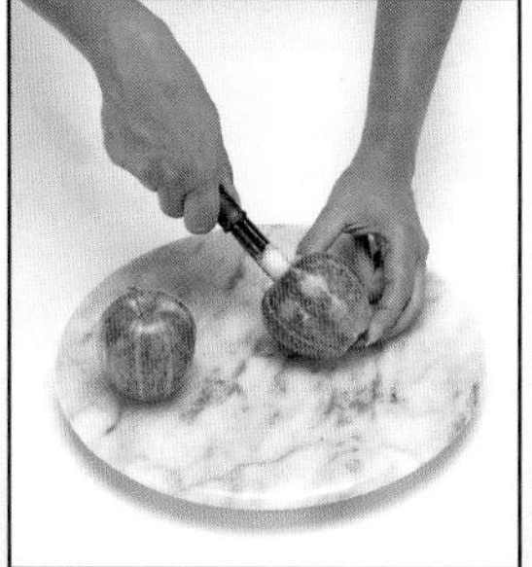

Wash and dry the apple, then remove the stalk. With an apple corer, push hard into the apple from where you removed the stalk. Push the corer through from the top to the bottom, twist it through 360°, and pull out a very tidy core. Then pour lemon juice over the hole in the apple to prevent discoloration before preparing your garnish.

Hot Daring Dylan Punch

Serves 10
450ml/15 fl oz tequila
300ml/10 fl oz Kahlua
60ml/2 fl oz rum-based coffee liqueur
1 litre/32 fl oz hot strong chocolate
500ml/16 fl oz fresh cream – to float
Glass: A large glass pitcher, 10 heatproof glasses or glass mugs
Garnish: Freshly grated chocolate

Pour all the ingredients into a pan or bowl with the hot chocolate and mix well. Serve hot with a cream float in each glass (or mixed in if preferred). Then sprinkle each glass with grated chocolate.

BARMAN'S NOTES

When heating alcohol, whether it is wine, spirit or cordial, it is important, if you wish it to retain its alcoholic strength, that you do not allow it to boil. On the other hand, do allow it to boil if you want to lose some of the alcoholic strength, but still retain the flavour of the drink.

When adding spices, allow them to infuse in the hot covered punch for a minimum of 15 minutes, preferably more, to allow the flavours to round out and mature together a little. This helps to produce a more fully flavoured result. When using spices always try to use whole ingredients rather than the ground versions. Not only are they easier to strain out before serving, but they also leave the drink clear, whereas the ground spices tend to cloud the liquid and leave a sludge at the bottom, and sometimes a film on the top of the drink where they do not mix in.

Warm drinks should always be served in warmed glasses or mugs. They can be warmed by immersing them in hot (but not boiling) water just before they are required. Dry them well before using. The actual bowl that the punch is to be served in can be warmed in the same way by immersing it in warm water.

Julienne of orange peel

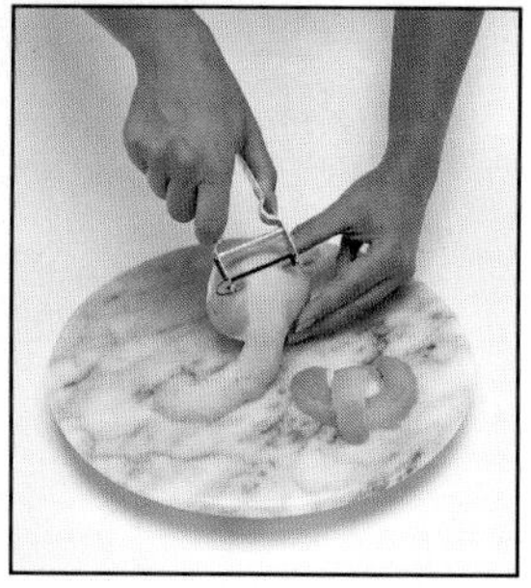

Wash and dry a smooth-skinned, brightly-coloured orange. With a vegetable peeler, remove a wide piece of orange peel from around the orange.

Cut about a two-inch length piece from the peel, remove any white pith, trim the outer edges to make a neat rectangular shape, and then cut the thinnest strips you can from the length of peel. This makes very fine julienne of orange peel for garnishes.

Halloween Raspberry Bowl

Serves 8-10

750ml/24 fl oz cranberry juice
750ml/24 fl oz rosé wine
500ml/16 fl oz orange juice
150ml/5 fl oz brandy
125ml/4 fl oz Chambord raspberry liqueur
60ml/2 fl oz crème de framboise
Ice
Glass: A 3 quart glass punch bowl, 10 wine glasses
Garnish: Fresh raspberries and orange segments. Orange peel twists.

Fill the punchbowl about one-third full with ice and add all the ingredients. Stir well and leave for thirty minutes before serving. Garnish with the fresh fruit and peel, making sure it is evenly distributed when serving the punch. For a special effect, float two or three large flowers on the surface of the bowl.

Staggeringly Scrumptious Coffee!

Serves 6-12

1.5 litres/ 48 fl oz strong black coffee (sweetened with brown sugar to taste)
300ml/10 fl oz brandy
250ml/8 fl oz dark rum
250ml 8 fl oz white rum
2 sticks of cinnamon
500ml/16 fl oz fresh cream
The rind of 1 orange finely cut into julienne
Glass: 6-12 heatproof glasses

Garnish: If served with a cream float, sprinkle with freshly grated nutmeg and fine curls of orange peel.

In a pan, mix the coffee with the alcohol, cinnamon and orange peel. Heat gently until hot but not boiling. Leave for a few minutes to infuse. Pour into warmed serving glasses, and float with fresh cream if liked. Add the orange peel and nutmeg.

BARMAN'S NOTES

Bowls for serving hot punches need to be heatproof. Do not worry too much if the only one you have is a kitchen bowl; it can be disguised for presentation. Wrap or tie an attractive piece of cloth around the bowl or put it on a tray and pile fruit and leaves around it. For example, if serving a punch for Christmas, surround the bowl with holly, Christmas roses, mistletoe and chestnuts. The Halloween bowl can be surrounded with fresh cranberries, evergreen leaves and orange twists, or just slices of fruit and extra whole fruit to serve with the punch – use your imagination a little! Hot punches tend to lose their heat very quickly, so another serving idea is to use a slow cooker if you have one, which will keep the punch nicely warm without boiling. If not, do not pour all the punch into the serving container at once. It is better to make a few trips back to the kitchen, keeping the rest of the punch warm in a covered pan on a low heat. To finish some of these punches I have suggested a cream float when serving. If you can get fresh double cream it really makes a difference. Pour it slowly on to the hot punch over the back of a teaspoon.

Low/Non-Alcoholic Sangria

Serves 4

1 (750 ml.) bottle of low/non-alcoholic red wine – chilled
150ml/5 fl oz freshly squeezed orange juice – strained
150ml/5 fl oz peach juice
75ml/2½ oz. freshly squeezed lemon juice – strained
1 tablespoon caster sugar
Ice cubes
Glass: A 1 litre/1¾ pint glass bowl, 4 wine glasses

Garnish: 3 oranges, 2 lemons, 1 lime finely sliced and halved, 1 peach and 3 apricots, peeled and sliced, 1 red apple and 1 green apple, skinned, cored and sliced finely, 2 sliced bananas

Pour all the liquid ingredients and sugar into a large glass jug and stir gently until the sugar has dissolved. Then add the fruit and plenty of ice. When serving, make sure that the fruit is evenly distributed.

Sangría

Serves 4

1 (750 ml.) bottle Spanish red wine, or any red wine available
125ml/4 fl oz brandy
30ml/1 fl oz Triple Sec
Soda water (optional) to taste
2 teaspoons caster sugar
Ice cubes
Glass: A large jug (at least 1¼ litres/40 fl oz), 4 wine glasses

Garnish: 2 lemons, 1 orange and 1 apple sliced finely and halved.

In a large glass jug, mix the sugar, wine, brandy and Triple Sec until the sugar has dissolved. Add the sliced fruit and plenty of ice. Leave to stand for approximately 15 minutes. Stir the mixture well and add soda water to taste.

BARMAN'S NOTES

Sangría is the Spanish word for bleeding, coming from sangre *meaning blood, or the colour of blood, as red wine is. In Spain and the surrounding area, it is drunk at many festivals with great theatrical drama – poured directly into the mouth from a long spouted jug. The art lies in being able to drink the Sangría from varying heights without spilling any! It has now become a very well known popular drink, cool and packed with fruit. Like many "convenience" products nowadays, it is possible to buy ready-bottled Sangría. It is made commerically in many parts of Spain – notably Tarragona – by mixing wine with citrus essence. However, the result is not nearly as pleasing as a fresh bowl of Sangria, packed with fruit, and prepared with your own hands!*

As I am deliberately trying to suggest lighter drinks throughout the book, a low/non-alcoholic version of the traditional full-blown Sangría has been suggested here alongside its more potent counterpart. Give it a try.

Tying a cinnamon stick bundle

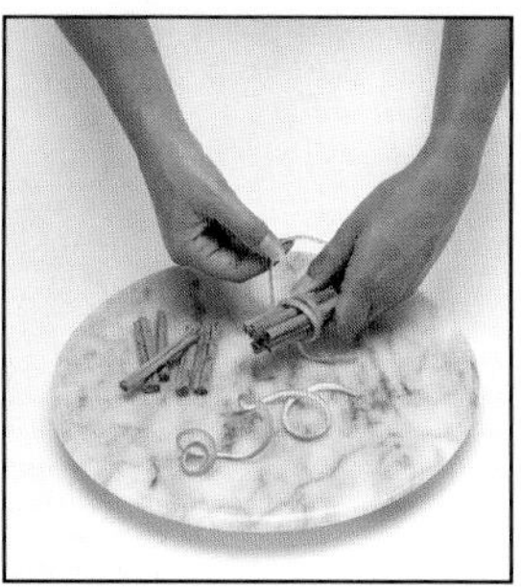

Choose a few cinnamon sticks of even size and length – between three and five sticks is about right. Then make a long canulated strip of orange peel "ribbon" from about half an orange. Hold the cinnamon sticks in a bundle in one hand. Wrap the orange peel "ribbon" around the bundle twice.

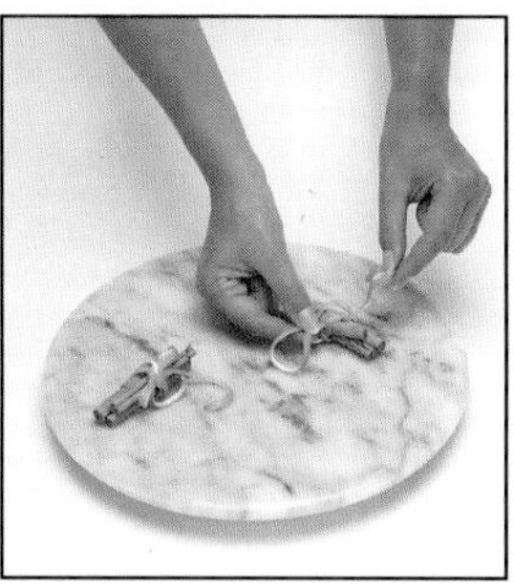

Finish off the cinnamon bundle garnish by tying the orange peel "ribbon" in a bow on top of the bundle. Use just as garnish in the punch bowl or add it while heating the mull.

Fruit Punch Mull

Non-alcoholic, serves 4
1 litre/32 fl oz apple juice
125ml/4 fl oz cranberry juice
125ml/4 fl oz pineapple juice
Juice of one lemon and one lime
2-3 tablespoons soft brown sugar
6 cloves, 1 cinnamon stick
Glasses: 4 heatproof cups
Garnish: 1 sliced apple, 1 sliced lemon and 1 orange segmented

Mix all the ingredients together and heat slowly, stirring until the sugar has dissolved. Remove from the heat and leave for a few hours to infuse. Bring back to a simmer. Remove the cinnamon and cloves before serving into warmed glasses with the orange, lemon and apple garnish.

Glühwein

(below right)
Serves 6
1.4 litres/36 fl oz red wine
125ml/4 fl oz brandy
30ml/1 fl oz dark rum
150g/5 oz light brown sugar
1 lemon – cut into six slices
18 cloves, 1 cinnamon stick
Glass: 6 heatproof goblets
Garnish: Slice of lemon, cinnamon

First spike each lemon slice with 3 cloves. Slowly heat all the ingredients to simmering point. Allow to stand for 20 minutes. Then bring back to simmering and serve.

Cider Mull

(*right*)

Serves 4

1 (750 ml.) bottle dry cider
A cinnamon stick
Freshly grated nutmeg and ground allspice
Approx. 6 cloves (to taste)
2 tablespoons orange blossom honey
Glass: 4 heatproof tumblers
Garnish: 1 orange, finely sliced

Combine all the ingredients together and bring slowly to simmering point. Do not boil. Allow to simmer for 10-12 minutes. Serve hot, adding the orange slices to each serving.

BARMAN'S NOTES

The origin of the word "mull" is uncertain. It possibly derives from the Middle English mold-ale *meaning a funeral feast. Semantics apart, basically it means "to heat and spice a drink", so under those guidelines anything goes!*

Ales have been mulled for centuries. Traditionally they were warmed by plunging a red hot poker into the liquid. Nowadays our methods need not be so dramatic. It is quite alright if the mull is simply warmed on the stove.

The traditional drink called Lamb's Wool, an ale mull which includes pulped apples, sugar and spices, was always served on the first day of November with sweet cakes as a celebration and dedication to the angel watching over the fruit and seeds of the orchard harvests. Its name derives from the words La mas ubal *meaning "the day of the apple fruit" and pronounced lamasool. Over the years this turned into Lamb's Wool. Glühwein has developed a tradition of its own amongst the many devotees of the popular sport of skiing. For some of them, a day is not complete without a warming glass of this spiced wine after their invigorating exercise in cold, fresh conditions. In Germany and Austria, it is also traditional to drink Glühwein at Christmas time – traders set up stalls in many a market square to dispense glasses of this cheering brew.*

How to segment an orange

Cut the top and bottom off the orange and stand it on a chopping board. With a sharp knife, cut away the skin and pith working in even sections from the top to the bottom of the fruit.

Take the orange in one hand, hold it over a bowl, and cut down either side of the natural orange segment as if cutting a wedge out of it. Let the segment fall into the bowl. Continue this process until all the segments have been removed.

Ale Mull

Serves 6

1.4 litres/36 fl oz ale
150ml/5 fl oz brandy
150ml/5 fl oz medium-dry sherry
250ml/8 fl oz water
125g/4 oz soft brown sugar
1 lemon – sliced
1 cinnamon stick, 6 cloves
A pinch of nutmeg and of ground ginger
Glasses: 6 heatproof tumblers

Put the sugar, water, lemon and spices into a pan over a medium heat, and stir until the sugar dissolves. Bring nearly to the boil, and then simmer for ten minutes before adding the other ingredients. Do not allow to boil. Serve into the warmed glasses. The warmth of the drink and of its spices is a wonderful antidote to the stresses and strains of everyday life.

Mulled Red Wine

Serves 6

1 (750 ml.) bottle red wine
150ml/5 fl oz ruby port
75ml/3 fl oz brandy
75ml/3 fl oz Triple Sec
2 cinnamon sticks
4 cloves, 4 allspice berries, 1 bay leaf
2 tablespoons brown sugar
Glasses: 6 red wine punch glasses
Garnish: 2 oranges and 2 lemons – sliced

Slowly heat all the ingredients on a very low heat. Bring to a simmer – do not allow to boil. Take off the heat and allow to stand for 15 minutes. Then serve into the wine glasses with the slices of fruit.

This mull is a really comforting drink for a cold winter's night, and excellent at Christmas!

BARMAN'S NOTES

In Poland, a country with a bone-chilling climate in winter, a mulled vodka and honey drink is popular. Serve it in small amounts as it is rather potent! To make it you will need:

Polish Vodka Mull

1 (750 ml.) bottle vodka
300ml/10 fl oz water
6 tablespoons runny clear honey
A vanilla pod
1 cinnamon stick
6 cloves
1 rind of an orange and a lemon cut into julienne strips
This makes enough for 16 small glasses or 8 mugs.

In a pan, heat the honey with the water. Allow the honey to dissolve before adding the spices, orange and lemon rinds. Bring it to boiling point, and then simmer for five minutes. Cover and remove from the heat. Allow it to infuse for at least an hour. Strain the mixture into a clean pan, add the vodka and warm through. Then serve.

Tequila Sunrise

45ml/1½ fl oz tequila
125ml/4 fl oz freshly squeezed orange juice (strained)
2 teaspoons grenadine
Ice
Glass: Highball
Garnish: A slice of orange and a cherry

Pour the tequila and the orange juice into a serving glass half-filled with ice, and stir well. Then drop the grenadine into the center of the drink and garnish.

Margarita
60ml/2 fl oz tequila
15ml/½ fl oz Curaçao
45ml/1½ fl oz lime juice
Ice
Glass: Cocktail, frosted with coarse salt
Garnish: A wedge of lime

In an ice-filled shaker, shake all the ingredients together. Then strain into the prepared serving glass and garnish.

Sloes in Heaven

45ml/1½ fl oz tequila
30ml/1 fl oz sloe gin
15ml/½ fl oz red vermouth
Ice
Glass: Old fashioned
Garnish: A lemon and lime peel tie, and a lemon wheel

Three-quarter fill the glass with ice. Pour in the tequila, sloe gin and vermouth. Stir well and garnish.

The Rising Sun

45ml/1½ fl oz gold tequila
45ml/1½ fl oz pisang ambon
Dash of blue Curaçao
Ice
Glass: Champagne flute

Pour the tequila and pisang ambon into a mixing glass with ice. Stir, then strain into the serving glass. Slowly drop the blue Curaçao through the center of the cocktail to achieve a very subtle two-tone effect.

Dodo

30ml/1 fl oz mezcal
30ml/1 fl oz white tequila
15ml/½ fl oz blue Curaçao
A pinch of icing sugar
Soda water or tonic water
Ice
Glass: Large wine glass
Garnish: Frost glass with blue sugar

Pour the mezcal, tequila and blue Curaçao with the sugar and ice into a shaker. Shake then strain into the frosted glass which should be half-filled with ice. Top off with soda water, or tonic water if preferred.

Chocolate Full Moon

70ml/2½ fl oz tequila
15ml/½ fl oz dark crème de cacao
15ml/½ fl oz light crème de cacao
30ml/1 fl oz fresh cream
Ice
Glass: Cocktail
Garnish: A pinch of grated chocolate

Pour everything into a shaker, shake, then strain into the serving glass and garnish.

BARMAN'S NOTES

Tequila and mezcal are both made in Mexico from types of agave plant. Tequila is a superior version of mezcal that can only be produced in two designated regions of Mexico. One is around the town of Tequila, the other around Tepatitlán in the state of Jalisco. Mezcal, on the other hand, can be produced in numerous places all over Mexico. Traditionally, an agave root worm is placed in each bottle which is meant to give strength to anyone brave enough to swallow it!
The very best tequila is called anejo *which means "aged" in Spanish. It is aged in oak casks for at least 3 years and connoisseurs will pay high prices, as they would for the best cognac in France.*
Tequila is made from a blue-coloured agave plant, mainly the Agave tequilana, mezcal from a variety of different agaves.
The mature succulent agave has all its outer leaves cut off before it is allowed to produce a flower stalk. The juice from the plants is fermented and double-distilled to produce a very potent spirit. This tequila, which is clear and known as white or silver, is the spirit that is drunk more widely in Mexico. For the export market, it is aged in casks or tanks to achieve its famous golden colour.
Traditionally the Mexicans take their tequila straight with a lick of salt from the back of the hand and a squeeze of lime.

Lighting Opal Nera

Like ordinary sambuca, Opal Nera can be set alight and drunk straight as a liqueur. Pour the Opal Nera into a tall slim liqueur glass. Light a match and hold it to the top of the drink to set it alight. To extinguish it, cover the flame with a plate or something similar. Do not attempt to blow it out, just in case the flaming liquid is blown out of the glass onto the table. Take care when drinking the Opal Nera, as it may be very hot.

Black Champagne

(right)

30ml/1 fl oz Opal Nera
Chilled champagne or sparkling wine
Glass: Champagne flute

Pour the Opal Nera into the glass and top off with the champagne. For a lower alcoholic version, use low-alcohol sparkling white wine instead of champagne.

Black Mist

70ml/2½ fl oz Opal Nera
A squeeze of lemon juice
Ice – crushed
Glass: Old fashioned
Garnish: A slice of lemon and a half slice of lime.

Pour the Opal Nera over the crushed ice in the glass. Add a squeeze of lemon juice and garnish.

Soda Cloud

30ml/1 fl oz Opal Nera
Soda water or elderflower "champagne"
Ice
Glass: Champagne tulip
Garnish: Lemon peel twist

Pour the Opal Nera over the ice in the glass, and top off with soda water or the flavoured water as preferred. Stir and decorate.

BARMAN'S NOTES

Black sambuca or Opal Nera is an Italian liqueur tasting of liquorice and elderberry. The word derives from the scientific name of the elder tree, Sambuca nigra. *Opal Nera means "Black Opal".*

The wonderful intense colour of black sambuca is achieved by distilling the purple-black elderberries collected from the elder bush together with an infusion of aniseed, lemons and elderflowers – the exact recipe is yet another closely guarded secret.

The better known clear sambuca is sometimes poured into black coffee. This creates a thin film of liqueur which is then set alight. It is drunk after the flame has gone out. Another popular flambé version is to serve the sambuca in a slender liqueur glass with 3 coffee beans floating on top. The sambuca is then warmed and set alight, and the coffee beans sizzle on the top. Again it should be drunk when the flame is extinguished and glass cooled! Be very careful how you put it out in case it spills. The Italians call this version "con mosche" – "with flies" – a joke at the expense of the coffee beans!

Making melon balls

Choose a ripe unbruised fruit, cut it in half, and remove the seeds. With a melon baller, cut out the flesh by pushing the baller into the melon, twisting it around 360°, and removing the melon ball.

Continue around the whole melon, knocking the balls out into a bowl, until the number required have been made.

Melberry

45ml/1½ fl oz Midori
30ml/1 fl oz crème de framboise
125ml/4 fl oz raspberry juice
A squeeze of lemon juice
A squeeze of lime juice
Ice
Glass: Highball
Garnish: A melon wedge and fresh raspberries

Pour all the ingredients together into the shaker. Shake, and then strain into a serving glass half-filled with ice. Garnish.

Abbie Dabbie

60ml/2 fl oz Midori
30ml/1 fl oz vodka
125ml/4 fl oz freshly pressed apple juice
Ice
Glass: Highball
Garnish: Slices of apple and a green melon ball

Half-fill the glass with ice, pour over the ingredients, and stir well.

Coconut Melon

45ml/1½ fl oz Midori
30ml/1 fl oz vodka
30ml/1 fl oz coconut cream
1 scoop of vanilla ice cream
Glass: Double cocktail or champagne saucer

Put all the ingredients in a blender and blend quickly. Then pour into the serving glass.

Green Gilli

60ml/2 fl oz Midori
30ml/1 fl oz kiwi fruit liqueur
30ml/1 fl oz gin
Dash of egg white (approx. 2 teaspoons)
Lemon and lime fizzy drink
Ice
Glass: Highball
Garnish: Melon ball and a kiwi slice

Pour the Midori, kiwi, gin and egg white into a shaker with some ice. Shake, then strain into the serving glass half-filled with ice. Top off with lemon and lime soda to taste and decorate.

BARMAN'S NOTES

This brilliant green, honeydew melon liqueur is becoming a very popular cocktail choice, principally due to its vibrant colour which enhances any clear spirit. It also has the added attraction of a subtle fruity melon flavour. These cocktails have been chosen to show a little of the versatility of this liqueur and it will also be found as an ingredient in other sections of the book. Other enjoyable cocktails using Midori are:

Midori Sour

45ml/1½ fl oz Midori
30ml/1 fl oz lime juice
Dash of egg white
Ice – crushed
Glass: Cocktail
Garnish: A slice of lime, maraschino cherry, and honeydew melon wedge

Put all the ingredients into a cocktail shaker, shake vigorously, then strain into a cocktail glass and decorate.

Melon Ball

30ml/1 fl oz Midori
30ml/1 fl oz vodka
90ml/3 fl oz pineapple juice
Ice
Glass: Highball
Garnish: A melon ball, a wedge of pineapple, and pineapple leaves.

Pour the ingredients into the serving glass half-filled with ice and stir well, then garnish.

Floating the cream

Pour the hot coffee cocktail into a heatproof glass, leaving a space at the top unfilled. Pour the cream into a small jug, position a teaspoon fractionally above the surface of the drink, and slowly pour the cream over the spoon until it floats on the surface of the drink, giving it a thick cream topping.

Crushed peppercorns

Place a few pink peppercorns into a small pestle and mortar and press down on the peppercorns, crushing them. You can now sprinkle them over the surface of a drink as a piquant garnish!

Iced Coffee

200ml/6 fl oz strong black coffee
2 teaspoons brown sugar
30ml/1 fl oz Cointreau
Ice
Glass: Highball
Garnish: Fine julienne of orange peel and slices of orange

Sweeten the black coffee with the sugar to taste. Add the Cointreau and allow the mixture to cool. Pour into a serving glass half-filled with ice, and garnish.

Frozen Irish Coffee

30ml/1 fl oz Irish whiskey
30ml/1 fl oz Bailey's chocolate and cream liqueur
15ml/½ fl oz Kahlua
1 scoop of dairy vanilla ice cream
1 scoop of coffee ice cream
Ice – crushed, ½-1 scoop
Glass: Large stemmed goblet
Garnish: Cocoa powder, chocolate sticks

Put all the ingredients into the blender and blend together on high. Pour into the serving glass and sprinkle with cocoa powder. Add the chocolate garnish.

Hot Coffee Comfort

125ml/4 fl oz strong black coffee
2 teaspoons brown sugar (or sweetened to taste)
45ml/1½ fl oz Southern Comfort
15ml/½ fl oz Jeremiah Weed bourbon liqueur
2 teaspoons dark crème de cacao
45ml1½ fl oz fresh cream
Glass: Heatproof

Sweeten the hot black coffee with the sugar to taste, then mix in the Southern Comfort, bourbon, and crème de cacao. Finish by floating the fresh cream on top. Drink hot through the cream.

Rosy Glow!

200ml/6 fl oz hot drinking chocolate
30ml/1 fl oz milk
30ml/1 fl oz dark crème de cacao
1 heaped teaspoon of freshly ground pink peppercorns
Glass: Heatproof glass or mug
Garnish: Sprinkling of crushed peppercorns

Mix all the ingredients together and allow to stand for a few minutes for the flavours to infuse, before serving. Garnish with the crushed peppercorns.

BARMAN'S NOTES

This selection of cocktails has been created to take advantage of some of the numerous varieties of coffee- and chocolate-flavoured liqueurs currently available. Added to coffee, milk or chocolate they are guaranteed to give "chocoholics" or caffeine addicts just the fix they need. If you are still not satisfied, here is another recipe to keep you going!

Mocha

200ml/6 fl oz strong black coffee
3 teaspoons drinking chocolate powder
30ml/1 fl oz Kahlua
30ml/1 fl oz dark crème de cacao
30ml/1 fl oz white crème de cacao
60ml/2 fl oz fresh cream or canned whipped cream
Ice
Glass: Large goblet frosted with chocolate powder
Garnish: Straws and freshly grated chocolate

Mix the chocolate powder into the hot black coffee and allow to cool. Add the crèmes de cacao and Kahlua, stir, and pour over ice in the frosted serving glass. Finish with a swirl of whipped cream floating on top, sprinkled with freshly grated chocolate and served with straws.

Pouring layers of a pousse café

A demonstration of the red, white and blue layering. For the best effect choose a narrow, straight-sided glass for this drink – this also makes it a lot easier to work out proportions to create even layers. Pour the "heaviest" drink, i.e. the grenadine, into the bottom of the glass, then "float" the next drink, the peach schnapps, very carefully on top by holding a teaspoon just above the surface and pouring the schnapps slowly over it until this layer matches the depth of the first. Repeat this procedure with the Curaçao, so completing the drink. It should remain in its layers for up to an hour if kept in a refrigerator.

Red, White and Blue

45ml/1½ fl oz grenadine
45ml/1½ fl oz peach schnapps
45ml/1½ fl oz blue Curaçao
Glass: Pousse café

Pour the grenadine into the glass first, then add the schnapps over the back of a spoon so that it floats on the top. Finally add the blue Curaçao in the same way.

Pomegranate Ice

Grenadine syrup (non-alcoholic)
Ice – cracked
Glass: Stemmed wine glass
Garnish: Short straw

Pile the cracked ice high in the glass, then pour in enough grenadine to drench the ice in colour. Hold the glass by its stem to prevent the heat of your hand from melting the ice.

Cool Mint Frappé

Crème de menthe
Ice – cracked
Glass: Stemmed wine glass
Garnish: Short straw

Pile the cracked ice high in the glass, then pour over enough crème de menthe to soak the ice in colour.

Olympic Flag

30ml/1 fl oz grenadine
30ml/1 fl oz crème de menthe
30ml/1 fl oz Parfait Amour
30ml/1 fl oz Galliano
15ml/½ fl oz black sambuca
Glass: Pousse café

Pour the ingredients very slowly over the back of a spoon on top of one another in the order given, starting with the grenadine. You end up with a five-layered cocktail, the colors representing the Olympic flag! To complete the Olympic touch, set the sambuca alight before serving.

BARMAN'S NOTES

A lot of fun can be had creating the layered effect of a pousse café – a drink made up of differently colored liqueurs of different densities. The sense of achievement when successful, and the gasp of appreciation from a surprised guest when presented with it make it worth trying.

A little preparation in advance is needed to make your creation work! Jot down on paper your choices of drinks, and then work out the alcohol by volume (proof) percentage of each. The higher the proof, the higher it will float. For example, a fruit syrup will almost always lie on the bottom of the glass, and a spirit like brandy or vodka will float higher. The Curaçao and fruit liqueurs lie somewhere in between.

The correct term for the different densities of the drinks is specific gravity, and it is by combining liquids of different specific gravities that the pousse café can be created. A steady hand when pouring the liqueurs over the back of a spoon on top of one another is also helpful! In this form they will keep in the refrigerator for up to an hour.

The other two drinks on these pages are frappés – that is, drinks served in glasses filled with crushed ice. The colours of these, as the ice refracts light through the liquid, are very spectacular.

Mango and fruit sword garnish

Cut a slice of a ripe mango and slice it into thin wedges. With a sharp knife, cut about one-and-a-half inches of skin away from the mango from one end of the wedge. Prepare peach wedges from half a stoned peach. You will also need two pineapple leaves, a yellow cocktail cherry and a cocktail sword. First thread the cherry onto the cocktail sword, followed by a peach slice, a pair of pineapple leaves, and, finally, another slice of peach. To assemble the garnish, stand the mango slice over the glass rim and then balance the decorated sword in front.

Ah!

30ml/1 fl oz rum-based coffee liqueur
30ml/1 fl oz Cointreau
30ml/1 fl oz Bailey's chocolate and cream liqueur
15ml/½ fl oz amaretto
Ice
Glass: Champagne flute
Garnish: 3 chocolate-covered coffee beans, orange peel spiral

Place the coffee beans in the bottom of the glass and three ice cubes on top of them. Pour all the ingredients into a shaker, shake, and strain into the glass.

Just Peachy!

60ml/2 fl oz peach liqueur
60ml/2 fl oz peach juice
1 ripe peach, skinned, stoned and cubed
Ice – cracked
Glass: Stemmed wine glass
Garnish: Kumquat slices

Put all the ingredients together in a blender. Blend until smooth, and pour into the glass half-filled with ice. Garnish by floating slices of kumquat on the surface.

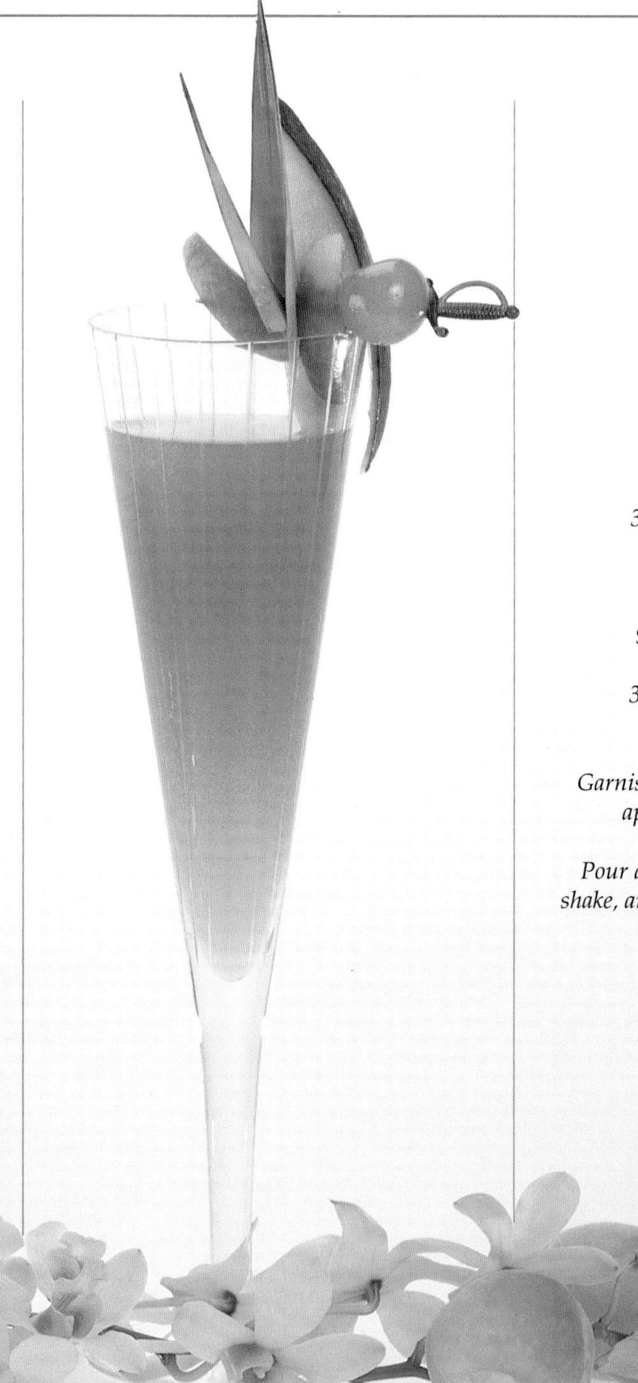

Boos Bonanza

Serves 2
30ml/1 fl oz apricot brandy
15ml/½ fl oz light rum
15ml/½ fl oz golden rum
15ml/½ fl oz dark rum
90ml/3 fl oz mango nectar
60ml/2 fl oz apricot juice
30ml/1 fl oz pineapple juice
Ice
Glass: Champagne flute
Garnish: Pineapple leaves, mango and apricot slices, cocktail cherry

Pour all the ingredients into a shaker, shake, and strain into the serving glasses. Garnish as illustrated.

BARMAN'S NOTES

These drinks have no precise international definition. Whereas in most other parts of the world they are called liqueurs, in the United States they are referred to as cordials. Many English-speaking countries think of a cordial as a concentrated fruit juice without any alcohol.

Liqueurs are drinks made with a spirit base of varying degrees of strength, and they encompass a tremendous variety of flavours and colours, and are generally sweetened. We usually think of a liqueur as a drink taken at the end of a meal, whereas in Europe they can be drunk at any time of the day, even as an apéritif before a meal.

There are many different base types of liqueurs and although there are few hard-and-fast rules concerning them, something worth noting is the difference between those simply flavoured with a berry, fruit or flower – for example, crème de cassis or crème de cacao – and those that are a distillate of a berry or fruit, such as framboise and Poire William. These tend to be more like an eau-de-vie or a brandy than just a cordial, which may have a relatively low alcohol content.

Inverting an orange

Choose two very thin-skinned, smooth oranges, one smaller than the other. Wash and dry the fruit. Cut off the top of each, and with a sharp knife cut around the inside of the skin. Then scoop out all of the flesh and scrape the skin as clean as possible.

Then turn the skin of the smaller orange inside out and very slowly and carefully ease it into the other orange skin – thus lining it ready to be used as a container for the cocktail.

Valentine's Cup

30ml/1 fl oz Parfait Amour
15ml/½ fl oz vodka
15ml/½ fl oz blue Curaçao
15ml/½ fl oz dry orange Curaçao
60ml/2 fl oz cranberry juice
Ice – cubed or crushed
Glass: Double cocktail or tall tulip shape

Put all the ingredients into a shaker, shake, and strain over ice into the serving glass. If using ice cubes, try making heart-shaped cubes, clear or tinted with blackcurrant, or with crystallized violets frozen in the middle. They add an extra touch to a lover's drink.

Witches Brew

45ml/1½ fl oz strega liqueur
30ml/1 fl oz brandy
A squeeze of fresh orange juice
2 medium-sized oranges
Ice – cracked
Glass: Use the prepared orange skin
Garnish: A sprig of fir, kumquat faces

Cut a quarter off the top of each orange and scoop out all the flesh. Invert the skin of the smaller orange into the larger one, thus lining it. Pour a little of the brandy into the orange skin, swirl it around, then set light to the brandy. This gives off a wonderful burnt-orange aroma that will permeate the cocktail. Mix the brandy and strega in a mixing glass. Half-fill the orange bowl with cracked ice and pour in the liquid.

Cool Sunset

30ml/1 fl oz vodka
30ml/1 fl oz grenadine
15ml/½ fl oz triple sec Curaçao
15ml/½ fl oz orange Curaçao
1 scoop of raspberry ice cream
Glass: Champagne saucer
Garnish: Rose petals and raspberries, orange- and raspberry-flavoured ice cubes

Put all the ingredients together in the blender and very quickly blend together on high. Pour into the glass with the orange and raspberry ice cubes and decorate with the rose petals and raspberries.

BARMAN'S NOTES

I have had fun in this section creating some liqueur cocktails for special occasions!
The Valentine's Cup really had to incorporate the scented liqueur called Parfait Amour, an obvious choice really as it means perfect love. The drink brings out the orange quality of the liqueurs and by mixing them with cranberry juice, we end up with a passionate coloured drink perfect for any romantic occasion.
The Witches Brew was created with Halloween in mind. The orange represents a pumpkin cauldron. Strega is the natural choice for this cocktail, as strega *is the Italian word for witch. This liqueur is reputedly named after an ancient coven of witches who used to drink it as a love potion. Its recipe consists of over seventy herbs. Just for fun, to complete the image, try making the little pumpkin faces out of kumquats as the finishing touch.*
The Let's Celebrate cocktail (page 104) was created to evoke the excitement of great festivities – engagements, weddings, graduations, births – any type of celebration.

Arranging a long lemon peel spiral

Wash and dry a smooth-skinned lemon. With a canulating knife, remove a continuous piece of lemon peel from the whole length of the lemon. Hold the spiral in one hand. Place a few ice cubes into a clean highball glass, and then wind the spiral around the inside of the glass.

Add a little ice after each fall of the peel to secure it, until the complete length of peel has been coiled with the ice cubes in the glass, ready for the cocktail to be poured over it.

Benola

(below)
60ml/2 fl oz Bénédictine
125ml/4 fl oz cola
Ice
Glass: Old fashioned
Garnish: A lemon wheel and a slice of lime

Half-fill the tumbler with ice, pour over the Bénédictine and cola, stir and garnish.

Let's Celebrate

(centre left)
30ml/1 fl oz Chambord raspberry liqueur
30ml/1 fl oz vodka
60ml/2 fl oz chilled champagne
Dash of grenadine
Dash of fresh lime juice
1 scoop of champagne sorbet
Ice – crushed, ½ scoop
Glass: A large goblet or a tall tulip glass
Garnish: A swirl of canned cream, fresh raspberries

In a blender, quickly blend all the ingredients together on high. Pour into the serving glass, and top with cream and raspberries. Decorate with bright tinsel sprays, sparklers, or whatever tickles your fancy!

Sloe Gin Fizz

(left)
45ml/1½ fl oz sloe gin
Juice of one lemon
1 teaspoon of caster sugar
Soda water
Ice
Glass: Highball
Garnish: Lemon peel spiral

Put the sloe gin, lemon juice, and sugar into the glass and stir until the sugar dissolves. Add ice and top off with soda water to taste.

BARMAN'S NOTES

Liqueurs are generally made from a base spirit, such as gin, brandy, rum, vodka etc. which is then flavoured by different methods with fruit, roots, seeds, flowers, bark, herbs, juices or peel. There are four basic methods:
Maceration *The flavouring ingredient is immersed into the spirit until the alcohol absorbs its flavour. This can take up to a year to achieve.*
Infusion *The agent is steeped in a heated spirit, which is kept at the same temperature for a few days. This method is more effective and cheaper than maceration.*
Percolation *Spirits can be bubbled through or underneath the flavouring agent so that the vapours rise and take up the essence. They are then collected and condensed back into liqueur.*
Distillation *The infused liqueur is redistilled, usually under a vacuum in a pot still. Some of the oldest liqueurs are steeped in history. Chartreuse, for instance, has been produced by French monks for centuries. The recipe is a closely guarded secret and is said to include 130 different herbs and spices. Bénédictine DOM is the world's oldest liqueur – the initials, incidentally, stand for* Deo Optimo Maximo *meaning "To God, most good, most great". The original recipe was developed in 1510 at the Abbey of Fécamp in Normandy.*

Melon balls on a cocktail sword

Prepare some half-inch melon balls from a ripe watermelon and a pink-fleshed melon. Then thread three balls onto a cocktail stick, alternating the colours.

Kiwi fruit slices

Choose a firm, ripe, round-shaped kiwi. Wash and dry the fruit, and cut it into thin slices leaving the skin on. The skin may be removed if you want to use the fruit to float on top of a drink.

Fruit Devil

60ml/2 fl oz raspberry schnapps
30ml/1 fl oz vodka
30ml/1 fl oz cranberry juice
150ml/5 fl oz raspberry mineral water
Ice
Glass: Highball

Pour all the ingredients into a glass half-filled with ice, and swizzle gently to mix them together.

Dingley Dell

60ml/2 fl oz peach schnapps
30ml/1 fl oz Malibu coconut rum
30ml/1 fl oz kiwi liqueur
Dash of blue Curaçao
125ml/4 fl oz apple juice
Ice
Glass: Tumbler
Garnish: A kiwi slice and a slice of apple

Pour all the ingredients into an ice-filled glass, stir, and garnish.

Peaches 'n' Pears

45ml/1½ fl oz peach schnapps
15ml/½ fl oz Poire William liqueur
Dash of peach bitters
60ml/2 fl oz fresh peach juice
Ice
Glass: Champagne flute
Garnish: A slice of peach and a segment of pear

Pour all the ingredients into a shaker, shake and strain into the serving glass. Then decorate with the slices of fruit.

Green Pixie

45ml/1½ fl oz peach schnapps
30ml/1 fl oz Midori melon liqueur
15ml/½ fl oz blue Curaçao
125ml/4 fl oz Aqualibra or similar herbal fruit drink
Ice
Glass: Highball
Garnish: Melon balls

Pour the schnapps, Midori and Curaçao into the glass, which should be half-filled with ice. Then top off with the Aqualibra and decorate with melon balls threaded onto a cocktail sword.

BARMAN'S NOTES

Schnapps and aquavit have a great history dating back some 400 years. They might be grouped together in the vodka family as they are also made from either grain or potatoes, and are then purified until neutral. The resulting base spirit can then be distilled and flavours added.

Aquavit is very popular in Norway, Sweden, Finland and Denmark, where traditionally it is drunk in small glasses, served ice-cold. In Denmark, herb-flavoured aquavit seems to be preferred.

The Norwegians produce an aquavit flavoured with dill and coriander that is a pale gold colour. Their famous Linie aquavit has to make an ocean trip to complete its maturing process! In the holds of Australia-bound ships, it ages in wooden casks. The climate and atmosphere on the ship are believed to help the spirit to mature, and to endow it with its particular taste. Then, on its return to Norway, it is bottled and the label indicates the name of the ship that carried it over the equator (the Linie).

Schnapps is more of a generic term for any clear, strong dry spirit. It is particularly popular in Germany, where it is available in a variety of flavours, the most popular being kümmel or caraway. By contrast, a more liqueur-like drink, peppermint schnapps, is quite popular in the United States.

Sieving fruit

Put the raspberries and blackberries together into a saucepan. Cook them slowly over a low heat, until the juices run and the fruits soften. Remove from the heat and allow to cool.

Press the cooked fruit through a nylon sieve into a bowl using the back of a spoon. Scrape the underside of the sieve occasionally to release the purée.

Blackberry Cobbler

150ml/5 fl oz blackberry wine
30ml/1 fl oz crème de framboise
12 raspberries and 12 blackberries – pressed through a nylon sieve to juice
2 teaspoons of caster sugar
Ice – crushed
Glass: Large wine glass
Garnish: A sprig of mint

Half-fill the wine glass with ice. In a mixing glass, combine the berry juices with the sugar. To dissolve the sugar, add the liqueur and wine and stir. Then pour it over the crushed ice in the serving glass, and garnish.

Saké Cocktail

30ml/1 fl oz saké
30ml/1 fl oz Midori melon liqueur
30ml/1 fl oz Russian lemon vodka
Ice – crushed
Glass: Cocktail
Garnish: A melon ball, a quarter slice of lemon

Mix all the ingredients together in a mixing glass. Strain, and pour into the serving glass which should be half-filled with ice. Garnish.

Iced Gold Velvet

125ml/4 fl oz bottled light beer – chilled
45ml/1½ fl oz chilled champagne
45ml/1½ fl oz natural pineapple juice
Glass: Champagne flute

Pour the juice into the glass, add the chilled beer, and stir. Finally top off with the champagne without stirring. To make a Black Velvet, use equal portions of chilled Guinness and champagne.

Belgian Raspberry Beer

1 (375 ml) bottle of Frambozenbier – well chilled
Glass: Tall beer glass
Garnish: Fresh raspberries

Pour the well chilled beer into the serving glass and garnish with the raspberries.

BARMAN'S NOTES

The choice of wines and beers now available is really excellent, catering to just about every conceivable taste. In recent years, brewers and vintners have provided the consumer with more and more options, from the aromatic elderberry, gooseberry and the very distinct birch and pine sap wines to the fruited beers made by the Belgians, flavoured with raspberries, cherries or plums.
For the more health-conscious and anyone who has to drive a car, happily the range of non-alcoholic wines and beers is on the increase. The improvement in just the last ten years is tremendous. A while back it was almost unheard of to ask for non-alcoholic wines and beers in establishments that are are now proud to advertise that they stock such goods and encourage the sale of them.
In this selection of drinks full-strength wines and beers have been used, but they could easily be replaced by low alcohol or non-alcoholic versions. For example, try making the Iced Gold Velvet with a low alcohol beer and a non-alcoholic sparkling wine, or even sparkling white grape juice and pineapple juice. Experiment a little, as the sober drinker does not have to put up with boring drinks.

Squeezing lemons for lemonade

Choose thin-skinned lemons as these are usually juicier and it is easier to tell if they are ripe. Wash and dry them before zesting or grating. Then cut them in half and push each section on to the hand juicer in turn, twisting it back and forth.

The hand juicer is designed to strain out any of the pips naturally when the collected juice is poured from it.

Homemade Lemonade

Serves 6

6 lemons
1 orange
250g/8 oz granulated sugar
15g/½ oz cream of tartar
1 litre/32 fl oz boiling water
Ice – plenty of cubes
Glass: A 2 litre/3 pint glass jug, 6 highball glasses
Garnish: Lemon peel spirals, slices of lemon, sprigs of fresh mint

First, grate the rinds of the orange and lemons, and squeeze out the juice. Put the finely grated rind and juice into a heatproof container, add the sugar and the cream of tartar, and pour on the boiling water. Stir well, cover and leave to cool completely. Then chill well and serve in long ice-filled glasses decorated prettily with lemon spirals, slices of lemon and sprigs of mint.

Raspberry Soda

5ml/1 teaspoon raspberry syrup
150ml/5 fl oz soda water or raspberry-flavoured mineral water
Ice
Glass: Highball
Garnish: Fresh raspberries and strawberries

Pour the raspberry soda into the serving glass half-filled with ice and top off with mineral water, then garnish.

Lime Soda

30ml/1 fl oz lime juice
30ml/1 fl oz freshly squeezed lemon juice
125ml/4 fl oz lemon-lime fizzy drink
Ice
Glass: Highball
Garnish: Slice of lime

Pour the lime and lemon juices into a glass half-filled with ice, stir and top off with the lemon-lime drink.

BARMAN'S NOTES

A traditional lemonade conjures up memories of hot summer days spent playing in the garden, broken only for a long cool glass of a refreshing drink. It is almost a must at a summer picnic, and makes a most refreshing change at coffee time during those warm sunny days. This recipe can also be used to make orangeade. Instead of using lemons and one orange, reverse the procedure and use oranges and one lemon. Serve with orange slices.

Fruit flavourings can be added to drinks to create very delicate mixtures, such as blackberry, peach or orange-flavoured mineral waters. Sodas flavoured with strawberries, blueberries, lemons and limes are delicious. Spritzer drinks can be treated in the same way to produce non-alcoholic sparkling fruit-flavoured drinks, like raspberry or mango and apricot. They can be beautiful, subtle drinks in their own right, or you can create new exciting flavours by adding them to traditional spirits as mixers.

Another nice cooling summer recipe using a traditional mixer – ginger ale – is to mix equal quantities of unsweetened apple juice with ginger ale in a jug with a good squeeze of lemon juice. Into the mixture add finely sliced apple, and stir the fruit, making sure it is covered by the liquid, then cover and chill. Serve in ice-filled tall glasses with lemon and mint.

Apple fan

Wash and dry an unblemished apple. Cut it into quarters and remove any core. Then cut three or four slices down the length of the quarter, leaving the top section attached. Spread the slices into a fan shape.

Pineapple, banana and carrot garnish

Cut a fan-shaped wedge from a slice of pineapple. Then cut slices from a banana, leaving the skin on, and from a peeled carrot. Douse the pineapple and banana in lemon juice to prevent discoloration. Thread the pineapple wedge onto a cocktail stick, followed by a slice of banana and carrot. Tuck in a little sprig of carrot leaf as a finishing touch.

Apple Cooler

Serves 2-3

500ml/16 fl oz sparkling apple juice
2 tablespoons of lemon or lime juice
125ml/4 fl oz water
30ml/1 fl oz caster sugar
4 eating apples – peeled, cored and diced
Ice – crushed
Glass: A 1½ litre/2 pint glass jug and large wine goblets
Garnish: A slice of apple

Blend the water, lemon juice, sugar and apples together into a smooth purée. Strain into a jug with crushed ice, and stir in the sparkling apple juice.

Pomme Noir

90ml/3 fl oz sparkling apple juice
90ml/3 fl oz chilled cola
Ice
Glass: Highball
Garnish: Apple fan

Half-fill the glass with ice and pour over the apple juice and cola. Stir and garnish.

Fruit and Carrot Cocktail

Serves 4

500ml/16 fl oz carrot juice
500ml/16 fl oz pineapple juice
1 ripe banana – sliced
A pinch of freshly ground nutmeg
Ice – crushed
Glass: A 2 litre/3-pint glass jug, 4 heavy-based tumblers
Garnish: Pineapple section, banana and carrot slice

Put the carrot juice and pineapple juice into a blender with the banana. Blend until smooth, then add 250g/8 oz of crushed ice and the nutmeg. Blend for a further ten seconds, and then serve.

BARMAN'S NOTES

Now the world is your oyster! In this category of drinks, the choice is totally yours, and what a choice! Almost any fruit you name can now be bought in juice form: bottles, cartons, cans and even in frozen packs, as well as "fresh off the press", where vendors will squeeze the fruit of your choice while you wait. With so much modern equipment designed for juice extraction – hand and electric juicers, attachments for blenders etc. – it is a pleasure to experiment at home, to mix and match your favourite fruits. Each recipe suggested here can be made with bought juices, but as a real treat (and for total healthy freshness) why not make the cocktail from scratch? Press the juices yourself, instead of buying them. It is a wonderful way of getting a good dose of vitamins. Soft fruits, such as currants and berries, are the easiest to juice as they release their juices simply by being pressed through a sieve or a food mill. This produces a pourable purée while separating out the skins and seeds at the same time. These purées can be drunk as they are, or diluted with still or sparkling mineral or soda water.

Fruits like plums or rhubarb need to be gently stewed first to soften them before pressing. Harder ingredients, such as carrots, apples or maybe celery, are best puréed through a juice extractor attachment which fits onto a blender.

Double orange twist with coriander

You will need fresh coriander sprigs, a firm orange, and a cocktail stick to secure the garnish. With a sharp knife, cut two slices of orange, tie them on top of one another, and cut into the centre of both slices.

Holding both slices together, twist them around to form an "S" shape, and secure this by threading it onto a cocktail stick. Tuck in a coriander sprig to complete the garnish.

Tomato Cocktail

(below)

450g/1 lb tomatoes – skins and seeds removed
2 sticks celery – chopped
2 carrots – peeled and chopped
A quarter of a small onion – diced
Dash of Tabasco sauce
A pinch of ground coriander
Salt and pepper to taste
Still mineral water – to dilute
Ice
Glass: Highball

Put all the ingredients (other than the ice and mineral water) into a blender and blend to a smooth purée. Pass through a nylon sieve into a jug half-filled with ice cubes. Dilute to taste with chilled mineral water and stir

Bright Eyes

(left)

125ml/4 fl oz carrot juice
125ml/4 fl oz freshly squeezed orange juice
A tablespoon of finely chopped coriander leaves
Ice – cracked
Glass: Stemmed goblet
Garnish: Double orange twist and coriander leaves

Mix the juices and freshly chopped leaves together in a mixing glass. Then pour them into the serving glass half-filled with cracked ice, and garnish.

Beetroot Juice

(below)

1 medium-sized cooked beetroot, cubed
200ml/6 fl oz mineral water
1 teaspoon finely grated onion
Dash of raspberry vinegar
A pinch of ground caraway seeds
1 tablespoon sour cream (optional)
Salt and pepper to taste
Ice
Glass: Highball
Garnish: Frost glass with celery salt, slice of lemon

Put all the ingredients into a blender, blend until smooth. Adjust seasoning to taste and pour into serving glass with ice. For a quicker version use bottled beetroot juice diluted with chilled mineral water.

BARMAN'S NOTES

Citrus fruits can be squeezed very easily with good results on relatively inexpensive squeezers especially designed for the job. To add a slightly more piquant flavour to the citrus juice, use the rinds as an infusion.

Excellent syrups can be made by concentrating the fruit juices and preserving them with sugar. When making homemade juices and syrups it is best to use riper fruits than you would choose for eating, as these will yield the most juice.

If you still lack the inspiration, time, or energy to produce homemade juice, just invest in some beautiful concoctions already created for you. The combinations of flavours that you can mix together is amazing. Try melon and passionfruit juice, or blood orange and raspberry, or cranberry and raspberry. And that's just the beginning!

Vegetable juices offer another exciting element to the equation – their rich colours are quite fantastic.

The recipes given here have quite a savoury taste; use them as a mid-morning drink or even as the starter to a meal.

To add a little pizazz to the Beet Juice, float a tablespoon of sour cream on the top, and drink the cocktail through this, savouring the celery salt frosting as you do so, as it makes a delicious combination.

Carrot and orange juice is another harmonious mixture – the chopped fresh coriander really lifts the flavours.

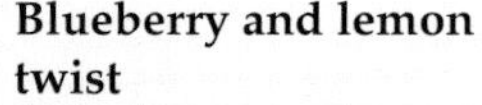

Blueberry and lemon twist

You will need a slice of lemon, four even-sized blueberries or bilberries, and a cocktail stick to make this garnish. Cut the lemon slice in half.

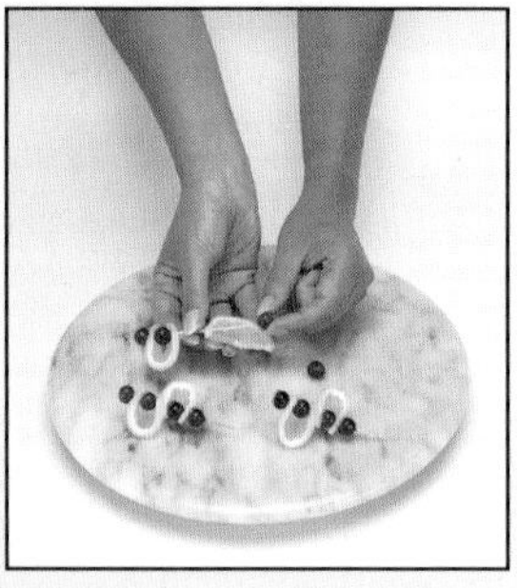

Thread a blueberry onto the cocktail stick and follow this with half a lemon slice, pushing the cocktail stick through the skin near the cut edge. Put on another blueberry and curl the lemon half around it like a sail. Then repeat forming an "S" shape with the two lemon halves.

Raspberry Fizz

(far left)

Serves 4-6

1kg/2¼ lb fresh raspberries
Approx. 90g/3 oz caster sugar (or to taste)
Soda water
Ice
Glass: Tall goblet
Garnish: A sprig of mint and fresh raspberries

Rub the berries through a nylon sieve into a bowl. Add enough sugar to sweeten to taste. Cover and put into the refrigerator for a few hours. Then serve in a tall ice-filled glasses. Top off with soda water, then garnish.

Blueberry Fizz

(left)

30g/1oz blueberries or bilberries, fresh or canned in their own juice
30g/1 oz blackcurrants, fresh or canned
150ml/5 fl oz blueberry fizzy drink or soda water
Ice – cracked
Glass: Highball
Garnish: A blueberry and lemon twist, a small string of fresh blackcurrants

Put the berries and currants into a blender and blend with a little water (or their own juice if canned) until puréed. Sieve the purée through a nylon sieve. Put the mixture into the glass half-filled with ice, and top off with the fizzy drink or soda water. Stir and garnish.

Cranberry Cooler

(below)

125ml/4 fl oz cranberry juice
60ml/2 fl oz red grape juice
60ml/2 fl oz lemon-lime soda
Ice
Glass: Highball or large wine glass
Garnish: Lemon wheel, small frosted red seedless grapes (optional)

Nearly fill the glass with ice and pour in the ingredients. Stir well and garnish.

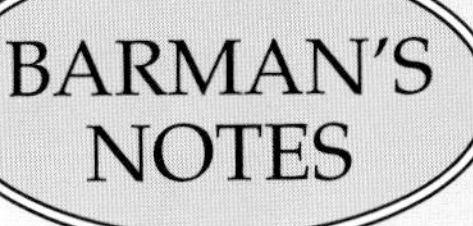

Cranberry juice really is a wonderfully versatile ingredient. As it is not very sweet, you can combine it in both savoury and sweet concoctions. Its beautiful clear red colour looks tempting in itself, adding a colourful zing to any mixture.

Fresh juices can be used in many ways, perhaps combined with one another to make healthy non-alcoholic choices, or mixed with spirits or cordials to create exciting cocktails, or even blended with ice cream to make some truly delicious combinations. The latter are perhaps a little high in fat and carbohydrates, but taken in moderation there's no harm done, so feel free to get creative!

Puréed fruit juices make delicious additions to all sorts of recipes – try exotic fruit or berry mixtures poured over ice cream, waffles or pancakes, and spiced with cinnamon or nutmeg together with a dash of a fruit liqueur. This can make a very simple and delicious dessert. Fresh pear purée, mixed with Poire William cordial and custard, and poured over a filo pastry frangipan (almond) tart sets your taste buds alive with its sweet freshness.

So next time you go shopping, buy a little extra for your fruit bowl, and indulge yourself and your family with a fresh concoction of your own making!

Strawberry slice with leaves

With a sharp knife, cut a slice from the centre of a strawberry being careful not to cut off the leaves. This slice can be balanced over the rim of a glass secured by a cocktail stick.

Strawberry sorbet cubes

Pack an ice cube tray with flavoured sorbet using the back of a teaspoon to press it down firmly. Put the tray back into the freezer to set hard. Use the sorbet cubes as an attractive alternative to ordinary ice.

Long Cool Raita

(right)

60g/2 oz cucumber, peeled and diced
90ml/3 fl oz natural yogurt
90ml/3 fl oz milk
8-12 mint leaves
A squeeze of lime juice
Salt (optional)
Ice

Glass: Highball
Garnish: A sprig of mint and a slice of cucumber

Blend all the ingredients together in a blender, on high. Pour into the glass, half-filled with ice, and garnish.

Virgin Banana Colada

1 very ripe banana – sliced
125ml/4 fl oz pineapple juice
45ml/1½ fl oz coconut cream
1 scoop of pineapple sorbet or 125ml/4 fl oz of canned crushed pineapple
Ice – crushed, 1 scoop
Glass: Large wine glass
Garnish: Frost the glass with dried coconut. A maraschino cherry, a banana slice, and pineapple leaves

Place all the ingredients into the blender and blend on high until smooth. Then pour into the prepared glass and garnish.

Strawberries à la Crème

8 very ripe strawberries
30ml/1 fl oz strawberry syrup
30ml/1 fl oz thick cream
1 scoop of dairy vanilla ice cream
1 scoop of strawberry sorbet
Ice – crushed, half a scoop
Glass: 2 tumblers
Garnish: Strawberry sorbet ice cubes, fresh strawberries

Put the strawberries into the blender and purée. Add the other ingredients and blend quickly together on high. Pour into serving glasses and garnish. Drink through wide straws.

BARMAN'S NOTES

These drinks provide quite a sustaining source of nourishment, as they use dairy products such as milk, yogurt and ice creams, and also ingredients such as coconut cream combined with freshly puréed fruit and fruit juices. They could really be a meal in themselves, and certainly make a healthy snack for children.

Fresh eggs can also be incorporated into a number of the recipes so making them into a thicker and even more wholesome concoction. When making these drinks, the art is to add a little of whatever you fancy – there are so many combinations you can use. You can be overwhelmed simply using the tempting variety of ice flavours and fruits.
When using cracked ice, make sure that you blend the drink for just a few seconds to combine the ingredients; otherwise you will end up with a very thin drink.
Always make sure that the lid is secure before turning on the blender. If you forget, the enjoyment of the drink may not be worth the clearing up afterwards!
Be sure never to use your fingers to push down fruit or unblended ingredients. Always use a spatula; the blades are sharp, and very unforgiving to probing fingers when in motion!

Chocolate leaves

Choose attractively-shaped, unblemished leaves, and wash and dry them thoroughly. Melt about 60g/2 oz chocolate and with a paint brush paint the chocolate onto the outer surface of the leaf, covering it totally. Put it to one side to set.

When all the leaves have been covered, refrigerate them for about one hour. When set hard, peel off the leaf from the chocolate. Use the chocolate leaf as a garnish.

Mango Lassi

Half a ripe mango, skinned, pitted, diced
3 ripe apricots, pitted
150ml/5 fl oz mango nectar
90ml/3 fl oz apricot juice
60ml/2 fl oz plain yogurt
Ice
Glass: Highball
Garnish: A mango slice

Put all the ingredients into the blender, and blend on high until combined. Pour into the ice-filled glass and decorate.

Choc 'n' Mint Coolie

45ml/1½ fl oz chocolate syrup
140ml/4½ fl oz chilled milk
1 scoop of mint ice cream
Glass: Large wine glass
Garnish: Mint chocolate sticks, chocolate leaves, and chocolate powder

Quickly blend all the ingredients on high and pour into the serving glass. Garnish with the chocolate decorations, and dust some chocolate powder on the surface of the drink.

Ginger and Guava Cocktail

1 canned or fresh guava, seeds removed
60ml/2 fl oz plain yogurt
60ml/2 fl oz milk
125ml/4 fl oz ginger beer
Ice
Glass: Champagne saucer
Garnish: Guava-flavoured sorbet cubes

Put the guava, yogurt and milk together in a blender. Blend quickly on high, then pour into the glass half-filled with ice and top off with the ginger beer. Decorate with a guava-flavoured sorbet cube.

Pitcher of Passion

Serves 8-10

3 ripe peaches, skinned, stoned and cubed
2 ripe papayas, skinned, seeded and cubed
750ml/24 fl oz passion fruit juice
250ml/8 fl oz plain yogurt
375ml/12 fl oz milk
60ml/2 fl oz freshly squeezed orange juice
2 scoops of dairy vanilla ice cream
2 scoops of passion fruit sorbet
Ice – cubes and passion fruit sorbet cubes
Glass: A pitcher, 10 large wine glasses
Garnish: Slices of peach and papaya

Put the peaches, papaya and passion fruit juice into the blender and blend on high. Add all the other ingredients and blend quickly. Half-fill the pitcher with the ice and sorbet cubes, and pour in the mixture.

BARMAN'S NOTES

The easy availability of nearly every fruit imaginable, in or out of season, has really spoiled us. We take it all so much for granted that sometimes we forget to appreciate and use the vast and exciting choices at our finger tips. Wonderful fruits available at the local supermarket include mangoes, papaya, guavas, passion fruit and kiwis, to name a few. All of them blend beautifully into purées to make the most fantastic concoction of flavours.

Even everyday fruits such as bananas and strawberries simply puréed with milk to make a milkshake are delicious, and far more nutritious than powdered shake mixes. If a thicker shake is required, add ice cream and crushed ice as well.

For these recipes, I have tried to include a mix of ingredients from the simple flavours of Strawberries à la Crème to the exotic Pitcher of Passion. They really are ideas to whet your appetite – now it's over to you to concoct the "rest of the meal".

Making a herbal infusion

Many fresh herbs may be dried and used to make herbal teas. Some plants suitable for this are peppermint, rosemary and fennel. Group the herbs into small bundles and tie the stems with string. Hang the bundles upside down in a cool, dark, airy place until dry.

Place the crushed dried leaves into a jug and pour over freshly boiled water over them. Allow to infuse for about five minutes, then strain the liquid into a cup. It is ready to drink.

Rosehip Tea and Strawberries

Serves 4

4 rosehip and hibiscus tea bags
1 litre/32 fl oz freshly boiled water
250ml/8 fl oz of hulled and quartered strawberries
Ice
Glass: 2 litre/3 pint glass jug, 4 highball glasses
Garnish: Strawberry slices and rose petals

Pour the freshly boiled water over the tea bags. Allow to infuse for at least 15 minutes. Remove the tea bags, chill the liquid, then stir in the prepared strawberries. Serve in ice-filled glasses. Garnish with strawberry slices and fresh rose petals, or even a small rose bloom, as illustrated.

Apple and Lemon Tea

Serves 4

4 heaped teaspoons of dried apple and lemon tea mix
1 litre/32 fl oz freshly boiled water
Glass: 1 litre/2 pint jug, 4 heatproof glasses
Garnish: A slice of lemon

Put the dried fruit mix into the jug, pour on the boiling water, and leave for about 15 minutes. Then pour the plumped-up fruit with the liquid into the mugs, and drink hot (without milk). Eat the fruit afterwards! Alternatively, for a cold drink, strain off the liquid and chill. Serve with ice in a glass.

Iced Peppermint Tea

Serves 2

5 sprigs of peppermint
500ml/16 fl oz boiling water
Dash of lemon juice
Ice
Glass: 600ml/1 pint glass jug, 2 highball glasses
Garnish: Fresh mint sprigs

Pour the freshly boiled water over the peppermint leaves. Stir and allow to infuse (ideally allow the water to go cold naturally). Remove the peppermint leaves and pour the cooled infusion into the serving glasses, which should be nearly filled with ice. Garnish with mint.

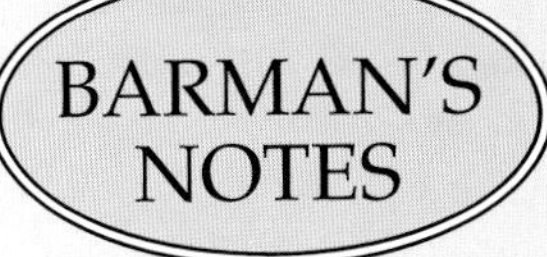

These three recipes have been chosen to show the different types of ingredients available. The peppermint tea uses fresh leaves. The rosehip combines a herbal teabag with fresh fruits. The lemon and apple is made from actual pieces of dried fruit combined with spices that can be bought commercially already made. All create fresh flavours and a caffeine-free drink.

Tisanes are a fragrant infusion of plants prepared in the same way as tea, and are generally known as herbal teas. These have become more and more popular in our highly charged and stressed modern world, as they contain no stimulants like caffeine. Originally created for medicinal use, they were sold by herbalists and chemists. Now they have become a popular everyday drink and are widely available in virtually any food store. They are normally drunk hot, without milk, sweetened to taste, but chilled with ice in the summer they are also very refreshing.

You can make your own herb tisanes from a selection of commonly available plants, many of which grow in any kitchen garden e.g. mint, sage, thyme, elderflower, chamomile or lime (linden). If you dry the leaves or flowers, it concentrates the flavour.

Index